STAND YOUR GROUND

The Self-Defence Guide for Women

with Khaleghl Quinn

IN ASSOCIATION WITH
CHANNEL FOUR TELEVISION CORPORATION

Pandora
An Imprint of HarperCollins*Publishers*
77–85 Fulham Palace Road,
Hammersmith, London W6 8JB
1160 Battery Street,
San Francisco, California 94111–1213

First published by Orbis Publishing Limited 1983
Second edition published by Macdonald Optima 1988
Pandora edition, revised and updated, 1994
1 3 5 7 9 10 8 6 4 2

© Khaleghl Quinn 1983, 1994
Illustrations © Orbis Publishing Limited 1983

Khaleghl Quinn asserts the moral right to
be identified as the author of this work

Illustrated by Patricia Ludlow
Photographs by Sue Adler, Gareth Redstone of Photo Design
and David Johnson

This book is based on the television series *Stand Your Ground*,
produced for Channel Four by the Moving Picture Company
Limited, and is published in association with
Channel Four Television Corporation

A catalogue record for this book
is available from the British Library

ISBN 0 04 440894 3

Printed in Great Britain by
Woolnough Bookbinding Limited,
Irthlingborough, Northamptonshire

All rights reserved. No part of this publication may be
reproduced, stored in a retrieval system, or transmitted,
in any form or by any means, electronic, mechanical,
photocopying, recording or otherwise, without the prior
permission of the publishers.

AUTHOR'S ACKNOWLEDGMENTS

There have been so many influential people in my life's development – an entire two books could be written about them – but, as it is, I would like to thank the following who directly helped me to stand my ground in this chapter of my life: my parents, grandparents, brothers and sisters for their ever-abiding support, my judo teachers, Kazuko Swauger, third dan, and Keiko Fukuda, sixth dan, for their wisdom and inspiration; Alexandra and Jon Kennedy for their work in bioenergetics; Doctors Ernest Holmes and Elizabeth Bryce Reed for their wisdom and work in the field of metaphysics; Michael Siegel for his genius in movement; Suzanne Gandy, Janet Gellman, Teri Schweitzer and Dail Groves for their assistance in my teaching; all of my students who have taught me so much in their growing; Ruth McCall for her warmth and the work she did researching for the television series; Judith Lowe of the London Women's Self-Defence Teachers Group and Ana Cooper and Jacqui Maskall for their tea and sympathy; Santa Cruz Women Against Rape for all their work and courage; Allan Tyrer for his delightful humour and his skill in editing the television series; Sue Adler for modelling for the illustrations; Maggie Comport, my editor, for her wisdom and sensitivity and for her work in highlighting and preserving the integrity of a concept of self-defence; and special thanks to Jenny Wilkes, director of the television series, whose subtle portraits of humanity reflect depth and compassion, and to Bradley Smith, writer and fellow-Californian, for being midwives to the television series *Stand Your Ground*.

PUBLISHER'S NOTE

Guidance on the law as to self-defence in England and Wales:
Self-defence in its physical sense involves force. Depending upon the extent of the force and the injury caused, the user is potentially liable to prosecution for a criminal offence including, for instance, assault, assault causing grievous bodily harm, and even murder or manslaughter if death resulted. (See pages 53-4.)

In certain circumstances the use of the force is regarded as being justified so that no crime is treated as having been committed. It is impossible to state every circumstance in which that is so since the outcome of each case depends upon its facts and the view taken of them by the jury and the Court. It is however possible to provide some general guidelines from cases which have come before the Courts:-
- You may use force if it is reasonable to do so in all the circumstances.
- The force must not be disproportionate to the harm likely to be done to you.
- If it is possible to escape safely or avoid the attack or injury without using force then you should do so.

If the reader is in any doubt as to whether the same or similar law applies in her country then she should make appropriate enquiries.

CONTENTS

About the Author 6

Introduction 8

ATTITUDE

*An essential reassessment of our
attitudes to self-defence which prepares
'us for effective physical training.*

1/ Redefining Strength and Power 14

2/ Self-worth and Intuition 20

3/ How We Already Defend Ourselves 27

4/ Fear as a Source of Strength 31

5/ Coming to Terms with Physical Contact 35

6/ Keeping Your Feet on the Ground 38

7/ Press-ups – for Women? 45

8/ Myths and Reality 51

9/ The Attacker Within 56

10/ Introducing the Elements 60

TECHNIQUE

*A practical manual of self-defence
techniques which explains how to use parts
of the body as effective weapons.*

1/ Agility and Stamina 68

2/ Using Your Body Weapons 74

3/ Tactics for Evasion 86

4/ Holds and Escapes 91

5/ Learning How to Fall 109

6/ Kicking to Effect 116

7/ Upper Body Strikes 122

8/ Throws 130

9/ Dealing with Knives 136

Phase 3
MOVING ON

A discussion on how our newly acquired confidence and physical skills can benefit every area of our lives.

1/ Where Do We Go from Here? 144

2/ Self-Preservation – a Necessity and a Right 147

FURTHER INFORMATION

By Maggie Comport and Nina Behrman

Self-Defence Courses – What to Look for 156

Self-Defence in Martial Arts 160

Avoiding Confrontation 161

Helpful and Campaigning Organizations 165

Child Abuse 168

What to Do if You Have Been Attacked 169

Pregnancy 170

Working for Change 171

Index 176

ABOUT THE AUTHOR

Khaleghl Quinn is a black American woman with a second degree black belt in judo. An acknowledged expert in the art of self-defence, she has taught defence classes to men, women and children, and trained others to teach such courses, for many years. She currently lives in London and teaches at her Quindo Centre there and in California.

Khaleghl trains women in martial arts based self-defence techniques, because she believes women can and should learn to defend themselves physically. She sees physical training as worthwhile because she knows from experience that brute strength does not imply an irreversible advantage. Indeed the martial arts rely on an awareness of the attacker's weaknesses, plus the ability to turn their strengths back on themselves. The qualities that a martial arts training instils are acute observation, judgement, determination, alertness, agility, speed and a degree of stamina – qualities on which males do not hold the monopoly.

She also believes that women are not as physically weak as they are persistently portrayed – and frequently believe themselves to be. This is why she feels it is not enough for women to learn to defend themselves with their bodies alone, they have to learn to change their attitude too.

These beliefs underpin Khaleghl's teaching that we already have the mental and physical resources to take care of ourselves. She shows women how to get back in touch with these resources plus developing them further. She does not work by instilling sets of rules, but explores with women in her classes what prejudices and preconceptions are affecting their ability to take steps to ensure their safety. Her methods digress from conventional self-defence teaching in that she does not believe that blind fear is the best motivation, conditioned reflexes are not her goal, and she lays great emphasis on intuition as a guide in times of danger, believing that, if we value ourselves and trust the messages of our intuition, it will provide a true protection in helping women to avoid confrontation.

This book is based on an eight-part series which she made and presented for Channel Four Television. In Phase 1 she prepares women mentally for the physical training that is to follow. She encourages us to increase our self-esteem, to place more trust in intuition, and to use our body language to reflect this more positive approach. Phase 2 explains how to use parts of the body as weapons in our self-defence and goes through a range of physical techniques. Phase 3 discusses how the development of confidence through changes in attitude together with the acquisition of basic physical techniques can lead to a deeper understanding of and resistance to all forms of oppression. As a result of working with Khaleghl's ideas, we can take stock of what we want to change in our immediate surroundings and develop the power to do something about it.

Khaleghl is a walking recommendation for the value of her theories. She radiates a calm self-assurance and dignity which instantly command respect. People who meet her feel straight away that here is someone with enormous reserves, with a quiet power and very low-key kind of controlled strength, against whom no manipulator or bully would make much headway. People also respond immediately to her gentleness, receptiveness, understanding and sense of fun and humour. She has great magnetism and everybody loves to work with her. Not everyone can be taught by her personally, but this book is imbued with many of her qualities and the reader will find it a pleasure to learn from.

INTRODUCTION

It seems that violence is an inescapable part of life. We find it in the world of nature, in the name of religion, on our streets and, sadly, in many of our homes. Domestic violence is on the increase, and runs rife amongst even the most educated. It is sanctioned by some cultural communities as a natural event in the institution of marriage. It is for this reason that Asian women suffer a suicide rate of three times that of women of other cultural backgrounds. Even after nearly a quarter of a century after the women's movement there are still those of us who commit *feminist suicide* by allowing ourselves to be brainwashed with religious morals that say we are less than man.

Then, of course, there are those unrealistic images of ourselves in the media. I remember reading a study in the magazine *Psychology Today* that revealed that over 80 per cent of women never mature in their physique beyond the equivalent of a twelve year old boy. It is no wonder why eating disorders such as anorexia and bulimia serve as so many women's disciplinary coaches. The twenty-first century is upon us, yet the spectre of the Neanderthal caricature persists in regurgitating its obsolete behaviour. No matter how highly educated a woman is or how high her position in society, women are still expected to be dragged along behind men by the financial hairs of our freedom and financial merit.

Any woman who has a healthy sense of self-worth and the courage to stand her ground in the face of menacing denigrating emotional impact of these live attitudes of consensus subjugation is usually socially dismissed as one who cannot be a real woman . . . one who secretly wishes to be a man. These attitudes which speak of an inherent hatred toward the female aspect of life can only mature into daily practices of violence towards women such as mutilating clitoradectomies, rape and murder.

After years of watching the news, women's roles in major films, and reading about heinous attacks on women and girls in the papers, one morning I woke up and realised how sad and helpless I felt. The more I learned in school, the more my mind was challenged to think clearly, the more I began to explore some of the potential of my body through sport and martial arts, the sadder I became.

Then it hit me several years later after watching one of my relatives wield abusive and sexist rhetoric toward his younger sister that something was seriously wrong with the way men and women are generally brought up to view themselves. At this point the sadness and helplessness rose up in me like a phoenix and turned these ashes of despair into rage. My once limp, helpless-ridden arms and sunken chest became buoyant with a fire – a passion to do something about it. Rage, which was once masked by fear and chronic respiratory illness, and stomach ulcers was to awaken me to a new sense of confidence in my own strength. No longer did I find it acceptable to find myself amongst those relatives or others who I once thought were friends who harboured demoralising belief systems which supported the subjugation of women, and the lie that we are inferior human beings.

At this point of blossoming realisation I had a black belt in judo and several years of college psychology and philosophy. Because of my martial arts training I was asked to teach self-defence at the University of Redlands and accepted this offer as a first step toward doing my part to redress the social imbalance that used gender as its scapegoat and its weapon.

As I began my research into the general view of what self-defence entails some years ago, I found these existing views to be far too limited for the way I wished to approach the subject; so I use the term self-preservation, which I feel takes the issue into a more comprehensive and realistic realm. Anyone who participated in this self-preservation method found that they had to *give up the luxury of being weak*.

It is difficult to overcome our backgrounds. From the time we are children, women are constantly warned of the danger of rape. Living with this threat can insidiously rob girls and women of their sense of worth and, thus, their ability to defend themselves. Indeed women may even have acquired an obtuse sense of comfort and security by dwelling in the expected role of victim.

Women are strongly encouraged to exemplify a type of feminity (convenient for insecure men to selfishly exploit) which keeps them in the role of serving others to the exclusion of themselves. Equally we perpetuate this dysfunctional lifestyle by developing a comfortable false sense of comraderie in encouraging other women to remain in the socially acceptable role of victim. "After all this is a man's world!" This is *feminist genocide* and is being committed not only by men who are attempting to disguise their impotence but by women who find giving up the luxury of being weak, for whatever the reason, to be too threatening to this false sense of security, especially when they see other women around them gaining more strength in their self-worth. Rita Mae Brown calls this behaviour amongst women and even some active feminists the "crabs in the bucket effect". This happens, she says, when one crab decides to leave the bottom of the bucket to get out of the confines of the bucket, and the crabs at the bottom do all they can to pull this brave crab back to the bottom of the bucket with the rest of them. This is the unfortunate bi-product of years of oppressive conditioning by insecure men who have used the advantage of their size and brute force "to keep women in their place". Living with attitudes such as these inhibits our ability to protect ourselves in times of need.

In my early attempts to break out of this social conditioning I buried myself in my intellect and, soon thereafter, into the world of sport and martial arts. I thought that by knowing a martial art, and especially having black belts, I would feel invincible and immune to any possibility of attack. Instead I felt more vulnerable than ever. After being aware of this paradox, and experiencing alternate waves of pent-up anger and frustration with tenderness, it occurred to me with the help of my judo teacher, Sensei Kazuko Swauger, that perhaps acquiring a black belt had given me the inner strength to become more human – to acknowledge my strengths and weaknesses, and to move on from here. Once I gave up the illusion that my training in judo was to be a cure-all and end-all to all unpleasant situations in life, I began to feel more peaceful, powerful, and excited about opening the door to exploring new avenues of strength and confidence.

Many women who are slight in build and have no martial arts training can and do respond to dangerous situations with a strength, confidence and mental clarity which seem to come from their feelings of fear and anger about the plight of someone they value, but how many of us would do this for ourselves? Could it be that we have reservoirs of power and strength which are alternatives to the competitive, bicep to bicep yardstick? It appears to me that we do. Often the stigmatised and familiar qualities of womanhood are the keys to our sense of power and success in the world: qualities such as heightened sensitivity to our environment and motivation just prior to menstruation, increased creative energy during and beyond the menopause, sensitivity to the emotions in others and in our self, a lower centre of balance in the hips rather than the shoulders, more flexibility in the muscles, and perhaps the greatest one, use of "women's intuition" – when we allow ourselves to credit its messages.

Women do have natural resources of endurance and stamina – women marathon runners are being increasingly recognized for their outstanding stamina and lasting quality. We have the ability to bear and deliver children: while most men seem very happy to continue to enjoy one-up-manship, whilst patting each others' backs for abusing others and taking life away. These violent acts require no strength at all – anyone can take life away with very little effort. All that is required to abuse, murder and maim is a strong and cowardly intent to express one's personal inadequacy in such acts, along with the hatred of others that such inadequacy breeds. The source of strength that is typically viewed and taken for granted as a mere biological function, giving and nurturing life – not for the qualities it requires, is a woman's strength.

So rather than attempt to change ourselves by becoming something other than who we are, why don't we begin the change and redress the miscarriage of power by reframing qualities such as sensitivity to others and the dormant strength we have within us from subconsciously living with the fear of rape and other violence from men into *a strength that goes beyond competing with men on their territory.*

We're sitting on an unquantifiable powder keg of power. Five thousand years of social, physical, mental and spiritual oppression is a great deal of force. What if we were to harness this very force that has been oppressive and turn it to our advantage? With a bit of skilled guidance this shadowed power could turn things as they are known now on their heads. It all begins with each individual woman. By our very examples, those of us who dare to break out of the confining and inappropriate stereotypes have started an irreversible momentum that is contagious to other women and some enlightened men.

No man has ever been able to control nature. In her inimitable and unpredictable way she always has the last word. Nature seems to have the best aspect of self-defence/self-preservation – *the element of surprise*, conveniently stashed away. Let us put our intuition to use in concert with our innate, unique physical power and very effective appropriate mental/physical/emotional techniques that begin in nature. Let us be as creative and unpredictable as fire; as light, humorous, full of perspective, and omnipresent as air; as solid, knowing and enduring as earth; and as fluid, versatile and strong as water. These are the basic qualities of being that are natural to all of us. Their unique expression is the beauty of our birthrights.

If we, as women, are to devictimize ourselves in our bodies and our environment, it is essential that we look at our attitude towards our resources of strength and give more value to the messages of our intuition that speak to our minds and the instinct that speaks through our bodies. This must be the foundation of any enduring self-defence practice. For to be free within our most basic territories, our bodies, our minds, our emotions and our intuition and instincts, is to have reached the dawn of our liberation.

It is within the very basic territories of ourselves that our hearts may find courage and our minds may find the peace that comes from understanding and from remembering that **we do indeed have choice.**

PHASE 1
ATTITUDE

'Self-preservation is ninety per cent attitude and use of intuition.'

1
REDEFINING STRENGTH AND POWER

'Self-defence is not something I'm teaching you – it's something I'm bringing out.'

The basic premise of my work is that we each have something very special and unique to offer and express in the world. I don't particularly feel that I am *teaching* anything but, rather, that my role is to assist people in gently removing and transforming layers of fear which may have fossilized the gem of uniqueness which everyone has inside. Through building self-esteem and other related techniques I encourage people to increase their awareness of their strengths and to learn to accept their limitations and areas of weakness. In accepting our weaknesses we can have something tangible to change . . . if we choose. I also encourage women to draw from their existing areas of strength to lend them support while they are changing the fear and vulnerability they may feel into areas of strength and confidence.

What Stands in the Way?

I believe that a complex of feelings of oppression gets in the way of spontaneous expression and, in fact, has the effect of siphoning off our energy; the energy which would otherwise be used to enhance our confidence and to make us more aware of our surroundings (people, objects and circumstances) and their influence upon us. These feelings of oppression stem from fear. They may range from associations with actual attacks, or their threat, to fear of social systems such as dealing with administrators in a bank or in the government, to our own thoughts. Thoughts often discourage us, such as guilt or, 'You'll never be able to do that . . . you're not attractive or talented enough', or 'Why didn't you defend yourself in a better way?' and all the other 'You should do' voices. Each of us has our own ways of attacking ourselves.

Admitting these fears is not necessarily an easy task and definitely doesn't happen overnight. However, it is always beneficial in that, through admission, we release tension; this gives us more room, more energy to be more of ourselves. And with a different attitude you may even have fun with this process of unveiling.

Attitude

Self-defence, or self-preservation, is about our desire and ability to communicate the value of *anything* that is important to us. That may include our bodies (especially as women, since we are faced with the threat of rape), our homes, families, children, friends, personal belongings, our dreams and aspirations, our culture, and community. Looking at it in this light can open the door to a greater sense of choices. It can also evoke an overwhelming feeling of responsibility.

Since it has to do with choice you may begin and end with any one or combination of the above. This is entirely and specifically up to you and must be examined, explored, and carried out by you within your own timing. If you start to feel the pressure of having choice and responsibility, you are beginning to experience the essential force and, equally, the potential power of self-preservation. Within the knowledge that you can make a positive contribution to the quality of your life, there is a whole other world – one which involves greater strength and confidence to move with your impulses, greater confidence to know that you have within you resources to deal effectively with anything or anyone who would attempt to interfere.

All of this stems from a feeling of self-worth, because in order for you to feel even the possibility of acting on your impulses, of doing what you feel is right for you, you must feel that you have a purpose for living, one which extends beyond merely learning to survive. I am aware of the external conditions and structures which seem to have power in dictating the quality of our life, such as economic situations, racist points of view, sexism, and ageism, but I feel that we must begin somewhere and that somewhere is ourselves – exploring our inner and outer resources to make changes.

For example, if you have been in a situation where you had to defend yourself and you feel that you failed, I want you to look at what you did from the point of view that, given all the circumstances surrounding the situation, you took care of yourself to the best of your ability at that time. You did respond. You are still here and what happened was a learning experience – a platform from which you can gain greater awareness, greater strength.

When you embark upon the territory of self-defence it is important that you write down what self-defence means to you, making this definition as succinct as possible. In so doing you are beginning the first step – taking responsibility for getting out of it what you put into it. Some of the things you might find yourself writing are these.

Self-defence means:
- having more confidence
- learning to be assertive
- not being intimidated by my boss
- learning to punch and kick effectively so that I can develop confidence in my physical capabilities

Have you ever run away from a situation? This is a way of defending yourself, too.

There are many possibilities; the main thing is that you remain true to your needs – there are no 'right' responses. It is only what is right for you that is right. This will be your personal goal and will serve as your point of reference as more of the principles unfold. Self-defence begins with your taking an active part in defining your needs for personal security and balance.

Strength is in the Mind

There are two major ways to express physical strength. One is resistance through contraction. The other is repulsion of conflicting forces through mental and muscular expansion. You may only gain understanding of the difference, which is quite dramatic, through actually doing the following exercise from the Japanese martial art, aikido. Find a partner to work with, preferably someone at least your size or larger.

The Resilient Arm – Part 1

1 Stand at arm's length away from your partner.

2 Extend one arm, palm facing up, towards your partner's shoulder, so that your wrist is resting on their shoulder.

3 Now contract your muscles as tightly as you can. Also contract your mind with the thought, 'I won't let you bend my arm.'

4 At this point, ask your partner to apply pressure to the line of your elbow in attempt to bend your arm. They do this by clasping both hands together and pushing down.

5 Do all that is within your power to keep your arm from bending. Keep this up for at least thirty seconds or until you are exhausted.

6 Now shake your arm vigorously to release the tension of this exercise. Take note of how this felt.

The Resilient Arm – Part 2

7 Think of something in nature which has withstood time and the elements such as a tree. What does it have that has enabled it to remain so sturdy? It has roots. Without tightening your feet and toes by clasping, simply imagine that your feet are roots. Equally, do not tighten your thoughts but keep them fluid.

8 Now imagine a great source of energy such as the sun. Tune into the feeling of its vibrance. Again, without tightening your abdominal muscles, imagine that there is a sun in the centre of your body, above your roots.

9 Next, allow yourself to imagine and feel the force of water moving through a fire-hose at top speed. Continuing to use your imagination, transfer this feeling into your arm.

10 Ask your partner to face you again. This time, you will not be viewing the exercise as a conflict between the two of you. You are to take on the attitude of it being an exercise in personal expansion.

11 Place your arm on your partner's shoulder and mentally collect your feelings of roots, sun and hose. Now ask your partner to apply pressure gradually to the inside line of your elbow – gradually, because this form of strength may be new to you which means that you should allow for some adjustment time.

12 As you extend your arm keep it long and your hand open. Keep your knees bent slightly so that you have a feeling of springiness in your legs. Instead of looking at your partner, which you may have done in the first part, look beyond them and imagine that this fast moving water extends as far as you can imagine – to the horizon of the universe. Again, remember that this is not a battle between the two of you but is a chance for you to get the feeling of expressing yourself fully. So the greater the pressure that is applied from outside, the more you are to increase the speed inside, all the while maintaining a disposition of complete serenity. See your partner *only* as feeding your current of strength.

11

What happened? Was the feeling in Part 2 different from that in Part 1?

The Resilient Arm – Part 3

Now exchange roles and repeat the exercise. Be aware of how it feels to be on the other side.

As I said, this exercise is from aikido (a Japanese martial art which focuses a great deal on the use of this resilient kind of strength) and is different from the contracted type that you experienced in Part 1. This strength is called ki and comes from aligning oneself to forces which seem greater such as the power of the sun or that of a wave. This power is accepted by the mind, generated through the heart and what is regarded as the centre of the body (a point a little below the navel and into the abdomen), and is then released to express itself at will through the body.

The exercise shows that what we believe, we become. It demonstrates the power of the mind and will. If you thought for one instance that your partner was bending your arm, it probably happened, because the mind and body are naturally in harmony. The body agreed with whatever is within our thoughts. So, if you had difficulty with accomplishing the second part you may either have lost faith in yourself and gave up too soon or you may have needed more time to allow the images to locate themselves freely. Do it again, this time with the other arm. See if you notice any difference in the confidence you have in either side.

After having done this exercise numerous times I always find that people are surprised that they have this other form of strength, one which allows them to be strong with a minimum of energy output and a peaceful demeanour. When I first tried it, I was surprised and relieved because it meant that I avoided that bicep against bicep form of being strong which I found limiting.

My confidence in this attitude to strength was heightened when I tried it out on my brother who is tall, stocky and captain of his school's football team. In the first part of the exercise he bent my arm with his little finger, so the effect of the second part was even more dramatic as he huffed and puffed in his attempt to bend my arm while I gained more strength with decreased effort. This was because, as he gave more strength to my arm, I was able to use it to my advantage. This really changed our relationship for, while he learned that it is possible to execute strength in a softer way, I learned that his form of brute strength would no longer threaten me. This is exceptionally important for women to understand because, as you will discover later in the book, we don't have to adopt the typical male version of strength in order to defend ourselves successfully.

This redefined and resilient strength is the type that we'll be using throughout our exercises. After you get the hang of this exercise with your partner, try it out with as many different sizes and shapes of people as possible. Use your judgement as to when you challenge yourself and when you simply nurture and strengthen what you already have.

2
SELF-WORTH AND INTUITION

'Until we feel we have a right to be here and take up space, we won't listen to our intuition.'

I have heard many stories of small women who have not a bit of athletic training finding superhuman strength to rescue children, husbands or friends in an accident. When they see people they love dearly are being hurt and may die, they find this strength. How is this possible when we are supposedly the 'weaker' sex?

It has to do with a sense of worth. When we feel we are involved with someone whom we love greatly, or possess something material which we have worked long and hard for, we see them as having value and tend to make an investment of our mental, emotional, and physical energies to ensure their proper protection and maintenance. As women we are encouraged and socially rewarded for looking after others first and last. Even the idea of making ourselves pretty is so that we can attract a man or get a job or be popular. Why not take care of ourselves, make ourselves attractive for our own pleasure first and foremost and then, if we choose, extend that pleasure to others? Perhaps we fear that this kind of attention to ourselves would mean that we are selfish and egotistical? Again, this fear stems from our concern for other people rather than ourselves – an extended form of our social conditioning.

In its extreme form this conditioning may prevent us from defending ourselves in a rape attack situation. Some women who have been raped have told me that they did have several opportunities to get out of the situation either before it escalated into something serious or while they were being raped but they felt sorry for the man or didn't want to hurt him or thought that if they gave what was wanted they would be left alone; or, because it was a brother, father, friend, clergyman, uncle, husband or doctor, they didn't want to humiliate him by calling attention to him.

Yet, in conveying all this to me, one woman in particular was turning red with anger as she related her 'sadness' at feeling victimized in so many areas of her life. When I suggested that she hit a pillow which I would hold she said that she couldn't because she would be displaying violence which is 'not nice'. I explained to her how we are conditioned to take care of others and how this serves to enhance a psychological bondage which inhibits our anger at being violated which in turn inhibits our power to act in self-defence. Her eyes began to brighten with a spark of recognition. Then she began to punch the pillow energetically and went on for about thirty-five minutes, collapsing in an exhausted heap.

She said that the rage which she had dispelled was actually the same that she had felt just before she was raped by her lawyer in his office but she didn't then feel free to express it. She hadn't felt 'it' was worth all of the trouble. I said, 'You mean you don't feel that *you* were worth all the trouble.' She saw my point and said that through releasing her anger she is more in touch with herself, more in touch with her sense of power and worth and would react differently if anything like that incident ever happened again. It is that sense of self-worth which releases us from the paralytic psychological bondage of our social conditioning. Just as women feel the worth of their loved ones – and so will leap blindly to their defence – so must we individually begin to nurture this feeling within and about ourselves.

What is Intuition?

As you have just seen, a low sense of self-worth inhibits women's willingness and ability to defend themselves. Most critically, it also acts as a block to listening to your intuition and so being aware of danger in good time. Yet self-preservation is ninety per cent attitude and use of intuition. As my intuition has not let me down and I believe in its power, I have integrated the recognition of, and reliance on, intuition into my teaching of self-defence – indeed it is an essential key. But what is intuition? The word has been given negative overtones of vagueness and feebleness, yet the dictionary says it is a power of receiving direct knowledge without rational thought and interference, that is by perception. It functions as an invaluable internal guide which tells us both where and how to move next – as well as how to integrate that particular experience into greater awareness of ourselves and our environment.

If it is such a useful sense, and can be so critical for our self-protection and survival, what keeps us from using it more? The answer is the same one as that which prevents us from acknowledging our self-worth – our social conditioning. Intuition is always there, but we have all these other messages that stop us from listening to it. Intuition is often denigrated and portrayed as unreliable in the following ways.

- Its workings cannot be scientifically analysed and tested, so it cannot be relied on. But the converse could equally be claimed – because it works, its existence is a fact. As this sense is, by definition, the sum of *subjective* feelings, thinking and perceptions, objective analysis is a pretty poor measure for its effectiveness.
- Intuition is an inferior source of information – something only hazy-thinking women value. Men use intuition too, but then it is typically called, 'ingenuity', 'brilliant perception and insight' – or even 'genius'. When women use it it is usually stigmatized, trivialized and dismissed. But, whether it is generally regarded as an inferior faculty and a load of old nonsense or not, we are still left with the fact that it is an effective tool in many people's lives. It is used to sense danger (often to an absent child or lover), to work creatively, or just to find your way around an unknown town.
- Intuition is merely flowing with your emotions. Emotions are somehow regarded as inherently inferior, suspect and misleading, though they are not necessarily so. However, while the ability to flow with your emotions is an essential part of intuition, it is far from the whole picture: intuition involves near instantaneous, unimpeded integration of emotional reactions, thinking and perceptual processes.

The dynamic process of intuition lies in our ability to open more and more so that we may listen to all these faculties in unison. If you are conditioned not to trust your intuition, its message will be impeded and it will *not* be reliable and serve you well.

Developing Intuition

As intuition is such a wonderful tool for our self-defence, how can we develop it? The quickest and simplest way is to give it enthusiastic attention. In order for us to integrate the power of intuition into our lives more fully, especially where it alerts us to danger, we must break out of our conditioning. As women we are taught not to trust our own judgement, that our perceptions are likely to be faulty and inferior. We must resist this pressure. Also, we are usually taught to be fragile, demure and self-effacing – to give others the benefit of the doubt. We absorb the general idea that we are not important enough to have the *right* to be angry and that, in addition, we must keep our emotions under control so as not to make unladylike scenes. But anger is a natural response to being violated or hurt in some way. If we do not have enough self-worth to express our anger effectively and direct it correctly as a means of self-preservation – if we hold it in – we will have difficulty both summoning and channelling righteous anger as a major source of strength. When the natural response of anger is not dealt with at the time of violation, it can express itself in destructive ways within us – self-hatred, depression, suicide and physical disease.

It is important to express any anger that you feel.

Not feeling you have something of great value to offer the world and so ignoring your intuition is also a block to using even well-learned physical techniques of self-defence spontaneously and appropriately. What is the point of mastering the art of judo, for example, if you are unable to sense when you should use it. Although you may not necessarily need specific technical physical training to cope with a potentially dangerous situation, having it can only strengthen and enhance your aptitude in self-preservation and will serve to increase your projection of confidence in your everyday activities.

Getting back in touch with your intuition is, after all, only a start. If you sense danger in time, you may be able to avoid or divert it, but you should be able to fall back on physical self-defence techniques to protect yourself. These need to be studied, valued and worked with. The bonus of this physical study is that, as you acquire a level of competence, it provides a feedback which further sharpens your intuition.

It is a good idea to learn techniques because these develop a body language that communicates your idea of self-worth – telling someone your intention in words only is rarely enough. I usually get my classes to do a simple exercise so that they can discover this. In pairs, one partner orders the other to do something, using the voice alone. Next they repeat the verbal order, backed with an appropriate physical stance or movements. The second method is clearly more effective.

When a woman comes across as silly, frilly, girlish and insubstantial (whatever her age or size), she cannot impress people with the content of what she is imparting, or make her wishes respected. She needs to develop dignity and a presence, to take up more body space and be able to stand tall and stay calm. Practising martial art techniques often effects a radical change. The awareness of posture and breathing, the improved muscular tone and co-ordination, result in a relaxed, confident voice and stance – which both impart a sense of your self-worth to others.

A verbal order is more effective backed by a physical movement.

Being aware of and preserving your uniqueness and value should provide the impulse within all the techniques and suggestions you use from Phase 2, and you must be willing to remain fluid in your choices within your methods. After you have developed a repertoire of techniques, you must above all connect with your feeling of worth and then trust that your brain and intuition will select an appropriate physical response. To practise a kick or punch without this emotional content is empty and has very little, if any, power: it is likely to lead to your becoming a robot who is unable to respond to the subtleties and nuances of any given moment.

This way of dealing with self-defence techniques is very different from the traditional 'conditioned reflex' response. I have talked with several martial artists who were unable to defend themselves when attacked – one, because they didn't listen to their intuition; two, because they were not attacked in a manner to which they were accustomed; or three, they responded only with the physical technique and were disconnected from the *power* of their emotion. Yet, I recently heard of a woman who was studying judo who repelled an attacker with the threat of thrashing him with her umbrella.

It is very important not to get locked into a particular way in which we feel we must respond, especially to 'save face'. People often ask me what I would do in certain hypothetical situations and are surprised to hear me say, 'I don't know,' or 'If I felt particularly emotional on that day, I might first start to cry, and then see where my tears led me.' I would actually *choose* to rely on my intuition, because it has always been right, and my confidence is based on this, as I explain in Phase 3.

Being really in touch with your intuition and relying on it has another aspect, too. We tend to make the assumption that attackers and rapists are strangers and outsiders when, in reality, statistics show that in a high percentage of reported attacks and rapes, the assailants were known to the women (Phase 3, page 150). This doesn't mean that you must go around being permanently suspicious of all the men you know, but you *must* trust your intuition if you sense any changes – in their general attitude towards you, or on a specific occasion. You will need to take steps in good time to make them aware of what you will *not* put up with, or to remove yourself from possible physical danger, or to use your self-defence techniques in a tight situation.

But, if you are serious about self-defence, and you want to be able to trust your intuition, a previously established feeling of value must permeate all concepts and images of yourself at all times. It must serve as the vanguard to all the activities of your life. Otherwise, there will be gaps in which you are vulnerable to attack.

The Quiet Place

When you come to learn self-defence techniques you will free a lot of energy, emotional and physical. You will feel very charged up and on a 'high'. It is very important to be able to come down from that at will, both between exercises and after a session. You can prepare yourself for this now by practising how to become calm.

Within each of us there is a place that provides the nurturing and support we need in order to grow, and make decisions, to give and receive love. It is the home of our intuition. I call it the quiet place. It is the place which supports all, knows all, but is attached to nothing. It can be the most stabilizing force in our lives. It holds everything in perspective: 'Many spokes unite to form a wheel – but it is the space between them which makes them useful,' says an old Chinese proverb.

You can cultivate and augment the quiet place by acknowledging it daily. All you need to do is close your eyes and ask for the quiet place to appear. At first, it may take a few minutes to get to it through all the noise inside your head, but wait patiently; it will come. It may appear in any number of forms. Each person's is unique. It may be a beautiful landscape, a clearing in the forest, a cave in the mountains, a room in your house, or nothing at all. It may remain constant or change many times.

One way to get in contact with this quiet place within yourself is through being aware of your breathing. Sit still in a comfortable position and breathe the way you usually do. Focus your attention on the rhythm of your breath going in and out but don't attempt to control it. As you do this, your mind will become stilled and you will start to feel relaxed, detached, calm, and probably rather happy. Another way of reaching the quiet place is to practise a meditation technique. Being able to contact this core of inner stillness at will and in an unforced way is one of the main goals of various forms of meditation. As well as having more spiritual benefits, settling regularly into this mental state allows you to tap a source of energy, creativity and bliss – to feel renewed. Or using one of the western methods of mind control – such as autogenic training, biofeedback, or relaxation tapes – to achieve deep physical relaxation may be the answer for you. Or this quiet place may develop through repetitious acknowledgment of it on a busy street. It is yours to find at any time.

It should be the place from which all technique comes. As it builds strength as the centre for all your physical movement, it will gradually become the centre from which all your emotions, thoughts, deeds and actions emerge. You will find the quality of your life becoming more harmonious, more to your liking, and you will find a resource of inner strength to deal with the crises and opportunities which are landmarks in your growth.

By sitting calmly you can get in touch with the quiet place within.

3
HOW WE ALREADY DEFEND OURSELVES

'We defend ourselves in many unconventional ways – surprise is the key.'

We can begin to free ourselves from our psychological bondage by changing our attitude towards self-defence and acknowledging ways that we have *already* defended ourselves. If you have been operating on the assumption that self-defence means becoming a speedy, invincible fighting machine, and that anything short of that is failure, please forget it. Because of this popular and narrow notion of self-defence, women do not realize that they are in fact constantly defending themselves in other ways. Although you may well choose to adopt trained physical prowess into your own method of self-defence, it is not the only way of dealing with an attack.

Given the view that *self-defence has to do with gaining or maintaining safety in potentially dangerous situations* – in your own way, at a particular time – here are some examples of unconventional ways in which one can defend oneself. These methods all worked because the women stayed mentally on top, none of them was what the attacker expected by way of a response so they were disconcerted, and several made the situation rebound on the men. They all succeeded because they used *surprise* in one way or another. You may discover that you have already employed similar techniques yourself.

Causing Embarrassment

After taking two self-defence classes, Janet went home for a family reunion. One of her uncles roughly grabbed her arm, saying obnoxiously 'Oh, so you're taking self-defence classes. OK, smarty, how are you going to get out of this?' Her arm relaxed as she replied, looking him square in the eyes, 'It looks as though my taking these classes really threatens you.' He turned red with embarrassment and dropped her arm.

Taking an Unexpected Physical Risk

Susan had hitched a lift and was being driven along a motorway when she spotted a knife under the driver's seat. She was also feeling increasingly strange about this man, so she asked him to stop and let her out. He refused. Fearing greater danger and deciding not to put up with it, she picked her moment, opened the door, jumped out, and rolled down a steep embankment, sustaining only a few scratches and bruises.

Acting with Cool Disdain

Agnes was exercising her dog one evening when a man leaped out of the bushes and threatened her: 'If you don't come in here with me and do as I say, I'm going to kill your dog.' She replied: 'You don't make it sound very appealing, do you?' Leaving him completely baffled, she walked on with her dog.

Appearing Disgusting

Fiona picked her nose in the face of a man who was about to attack her late one night on the tube. He said, 'You're disgusting!' and went off.

Jeopardising Property

Lisa was being driven down a country road by a man she had just met. He had invited her for a friendly ride in his fancy new car, then started making allusions to violent and lewd things that he was going to do to her. She pretended she was about to be sick. He was so concerned at the idea of her throwing up all over his precious new car that he pulled over and asked her to get out.

Causing a Scene

Angela and Sarah were in their home one night, watching television, when a hooded man with a knife appeared in the doorway and threatened to rape both of them. Angela put her hands up, communicating to him that she was really afraid so that he wouldn't feel the need to continually brandish the knife. He seemed thrown for a bit and at that moment she felt her anger turning into power. Sarah had used her intuition to pick when to let the blind up carefully. Then, at the moment the man became distracted, Angela picked up a nearby small table and sent it crashing through the window to call attention to their situation. The man dashed out of the house.

Switching Roles

Evelyn and I were chatting in a restaurant one evening when four drunken men approached us. My friend is the director of a toddler care centre and has also assisted me in teaching self-defence. She is very articulate and has no qualms about speaking aloud in public so she told them to leave us alone. They did so, but after a few minutes they were back again, looming drunkenly over us. This time she directed them in a very motherly way, 'Go home right now. You just go home.' They waddled away through the door as though they were following an imaginary parent.

Low-key Ridiculing

A man on the tube was exposing himself. The young women nearest to him were turning away with disgust and embarrassment when, finally, an older woman peered over and piped up with, 'I should put that away, sonny. It might catch cold.' He did, and got off at the next stop.

Using Verbal Assertion

Pam came to her car after work to find a man in the back seat. She is confident in her use of physical self-defence techniques but on this particular evening didn't feel like fighting, even though she was very angry. Instead, she opened the back door and yelled at him that if he wasn't out of sight by the time she counted to ten he would be in serious trouble. He disappeared.

So, as you can see, there are no set rules as to how you should take care of yourself when you feel that your balance and sense of well-being has been upset. There are ways to be discovered and ones which may never be repeated. Many concepts, principles, and techniques may be learned, but when it comes down to it only you can know and judge what is an appropriate means of protection within a given situation.

In any case, I feel that it is important to acknowledge

all the ways that you have either prevented a dangerous situation or how you got out of one. Even though you may not be totally pleased with the ways by which you may have accomplished this, I should like you to withhold judgement at this point and see those ways as a beginning. Self-defence is not a new concept for any of us. It is more of a catalyst for us to increase our awareness of ways we have taken care of ourselves and opens the door for us to expand and strengthen our capabilities in all areas.

As you strengthen your awareness of your capabilities, share this attitude with others, especially other women, and encourage them in the ways that they have survived. In so doing you will be exchanging stories and ever-broadening your choices. Nurturing each other's strengths in a communal way is very valuable because it means that we can teach each other rather than always relying upon a teacher for confidence. You needn't worry that this will produce a false sense of confidence because your sharing is based on what has worked.

Through exchanging stories, women can discover various ways they have already acted to survive.

4
FEAR AS A SOURCE OF STRENGTH

'It is all right to feel and express strong emotions – they can be a source of power.'

As you are beginning to delve into the ways that you've taken care of yourself it is perfectly natural and healthy for you to experience *fear*. I want to make it clear that, unlike the line taken in many self-defence classes I have observed, I do not believe fear is the best motivator in getting women to learn to defend themselves. Many drop out of classes at an early phase because their fear escalates to the point of over-riding any of the strength they gain, and because there is no room within the course or the teacher's perspective for this fear to be expressed. It is often suppressed by the teacher with such comments as, 'You mustn't show fear because rapist can sense it, like an animal, and will go for you even quicker.' This rigid, 'stiff upper lip' conditioning often makes it difficult for people to express the full range of their emotional fibre. When people do complete this kind of course they are often very tense in their bodies, very limited in their view of a range of possible protective measures.

It is quite all right to feel strong emotions: they can be a source of power. The attitude towards fear, which says you must suppress it at all costs and, yet, must learn to protect yourself as a result of it, comes from a lack of understanding of its full potential. Besides the frightening images fear can conjure up, it is an emotion of excitement which means it is a source of energy. If you choose to look at it this way it will act as a trigger to the surge of strength and energy that you need to deal effectively with any kind of difficulty.

Holding fear inside or pretending that it doesn't exist produces its worst effect – paralysis. Just as you experienced the limitations of the contraction-resistance type of strength in the resilient arm exercise (page 17), the same holds true of fear which is masked as strength. It may work sometimes, but is by nature quite brittle and will crack in time – not to mention the rigidifying effects it will have upon your body, making you useless before that point has been reached physiologically.

We can learn a lot from animals about fear. When they are frightened they don't try to be 'cool' about it. They tremble which is a form of action. Any form of action helps to bring out strength and is better than freezing up. Then they are able to do something about the situation, whether it be running away or fighting or even a combination of the two. You, too, can learn *actively* to take the reins of fear into your hands and use it to your advantage rather than to your detriment.

Perhaps you are having a fear *about* fear: 'If I confront my fears I will be indulging in them and will become weaker and more vulnerable as a result.' This is a natural concern which crops up over and over again as we begin to uncover the attitudes and things that interfere with our feeling of being dynamic and confident in the world. By noting what functions fear can serve and by asking which one is operating for you at the time, you can tune into your resources to determine what to do next.

Feeling fear can serve one of five functions. One, it signals the possibility of danger. Two, it reminds you that there are elements within the present which were once signals of danger in the past. Three, it is a natural sign that you are dealing with the unknown and change. In dealing with the unknown we expand our field of knowledge which means growth, and growth always means a change of some sort – either letting go of an old way of being or expanding it – and this change can sometimes be a painful experience but is invariably rewarding. Four, it can be an indicator that you are not ready to take the consequences of becoming strong, to give up the luxury of being weak, which means accepting full responsibility for yourself – something many women fear. Five, what seems like fear can actually be the

Acknowledging your fear is a positive step to utilising it.

wrappings on the package of *reluctant* curiosity. I have a feeling that many of the things which disturb and alarm us the most hold for us an inevitable fascination and are actually clues about our true nature which we would do well to pursue. Whatever their source, I am not suggesting that you go out and confront all of your fears at once, rather that, when you feel your stomach tightening, your spine becoming rigid, your shoulders rising to your ears, cold hands and feet, your jaw tightening, and a feeling of being cut off from the strength and support of your legs, you ask yourself:
- Am I in danger?
- Are there elements within this situation which signal danger from the past?
- Am I having a natural response to the challenge of the unknown?
- Am I afraid of being successful in this situation?
- Is this something or someone that holds a reluctant fascination for me and am I actually curious?

It is possible to respond intelligently to fear. When we treat it as an ally – a resource for greater self-awareness rather than as an enemy to be beaten down or ignored, it serves as a source of strength and energy to do what we must to regain our sense of balance and well-being.

It is only when fear is suppressed, ignored, or in the case of its third and fourth elements, when it is projected onto someone or something else, that it is dangerous. Most violence, prejudice and hatred are motivated by fear – fear of the unknown, of difference, and/or the parts of ourselves that we fear projected onto others. This is one of the major reasons that it must be understood and brought out into the open with loving support from either ourselves and/or others such as family, friends, or sometimes therapists, especially those whose methods incorporate bodywork.

Fear is a powerful emotion – ignored, it will foster aggression which may be inappropriately directed outward onto others or back onto ourselves, breaking down our confidence and even causing disease. Confronting small fears (whatever that means to you) gives you more confidence in dealing with greater ones and releases that wasted energy into more constructive avenues, such as creativity or making life's dreams come true.

To Help You Confront Known Fears

- Approach fear from a place of comfort rather than from one of insecurity.
- One of the major reasons for confronting fear is to increase awareness so that you increase your sense of choice and, therefore, your mobility in the world. So it is counter-productive to *force* yourself to deal with your fears. This will produce resistance and yield only temporary results.
- Absorb and incorporate this information about fear *in your own time* – realize that any awareness of fear as a source of strength will increase your ability to absorb the other principles and techniques of self-defence/self-preservation.

When you come to practise self-defence techniques, always mentally prepare a realistic atmosphere of danger (real to you, in which you genuinely feel afraid). This will be of the greatest use to you in the long run, and will accelerate your inner strengthening process, and hence, your self-confidence and self-esteem. Allow fear and feelings of helplessness to emerge. The work of moving through and transforming these barriers into areas of strength will yield the greater satisfaction you will feel in yourself. Taking the risk, putting yourself on the line', in relation to your understanding of this action's importance for your growth, will ultimately connect you with your, possibly repressed, knowledge that you can have control within your life. This will help you start shedding the layers of being a victim and emerge into your radiant, powerful self.

5
COMING TO TERMS WITH PHYSICAL CONTACT

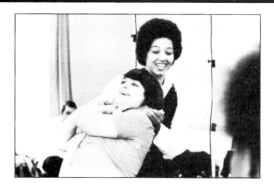

*'Comfort with physical contact –
with someone's body or their presence
– is basic to self-defence.'*

Most of the disorientation that occurs during and after a physical or verbal attack comes from the surprise of *sudden* contact with another person. This surprise is especially imposing if you are not accustomed to touching or being touched. Also, if you have the habit of relying on others to initiate action in both your social activities with other people and for your sense of value, it is likely that your self-esteem could be severely damaged by such an action.

When you learn the art of physical protection, comfort with physical contact is a basic. We must realize, though, that physical contact usually begins the moment we encounter the *physique* of another person. This could be someone walking down the street or someone who just entered the room you are in. When you practise awareness, it is necessary to amplify all of the senses so that intimate contact is maintained with your environment.

How do you respond to strangers? Do you look them in the eyes or look away? Do you smile nervously or maintain your natural state? Do this exercise with a partner, and you can find out whether or not you are at ease with who you are in your surroundings.

Being Touched – Part 1

1 Have your partner enter a room that you are in and gaze at you without speaking.

2 Now your partner will make a comment of their opinion of you.

3 Partner grabs your hand.

4 Partner grabs your hand and stares you in the eyes.

5 Partner hugs you.

6 Partner pushes you around in a bullying manner.

7 Lie down. Partner straddles you and pins your arms down.

8 How did each of these confrontations feel to you? Were some more threatening than others? If yes, which ones? Why? When your partner entered the room, did you feel that you had to entertain them? Did you feel self-conscious?

9 Change roles. Did your thoughts change?

10 While the thoughts are fresh in your mind, ask yourself the following questions:

Be aware of how it feels to be in the role of both attacker and victim.

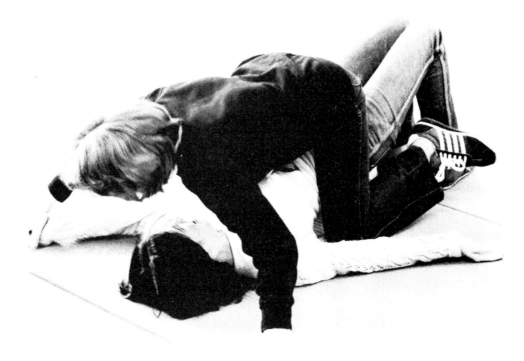

- When your partner made the comment about you, did you feel they had discovered something you had not kept a secret? Did you feel that they were right?
- When your hand was grabbed, did you feel that you should respond immediately? Did you feel trapped?
- When they grabbed your hand and stared you in the eyes, did you feel helpless?
- When you were hugged, did you feel gratitude?
- When your partner pushed you, did you feel a surge of rage, but that you were unable to change the situation?
- When you were being straddled on the ground, did you feel that you might not survive? Did you feel that any attempts you made to break free would only make the situation worse? Did you want to avoid hurting this person?

If your answer is yes to any of these questions, this is an indication that you get unbalanced by physical contact. The next part of this exercise will strengthen your balance while in the presence of a stranger, or anyone who seems to overpower you.

Being Touched – Part 2

Have your partner repeat steps 1 and 2. This time after each one, think about what is really going on, and say it out loud. Make sure that your voice is coming from your feet, stomach and chest, rather than from your head and throat. For instance, in step 1, when the person enters the room, you might say: 'A person has just entered the room. *I am myself* standing and watching.' Or 'I am myself with my feet on the ground.' Make a simple statement about what is happening to you.

Many times when people are grabbed or pinned down, they feel it necessary to react immediately for fear that they will not survive. In steps 2–7, where your body is actually being touched, grabbed or pushed, pause for several seconds, tune into the quiet place (see page 25), experience the contact and acknowledge the fact that you are still alive with all of your faculties intact. Then decide whether you want to do anything about it. As you get comfortable with more contact, ask heavier people to sit on you, stronger people to grab you. Doing this will boost your confidence. If you had once viewed yourself as a frail or weak person, you will begin to know that, by staying in touch with yourself under circumstances where pressure or heaviness is involved, you can be strong and cope. These attitudes can be used to cope with depression and social oppression as well.

6
KEEPING YOUR FEET ON THE GROUND

'The earth is a source of stability, as our bodies can be if we respect them.'

Now you are aware of your flexible strength, a sense of worth, your trust in your intuition, your intelligent mainline into fear, your faith in your ability to defend yourself, how do you maintain them? To do so you must feel a connection with something solid. Familiar phrases such as 'I was swept off my feet' and 'I was glued to the spot', 'She doesn't have a leg to stand on' all have something in common – an acknowledgement of the value and importance of the earth, of touching a base or the lack of one. The earth is a source of stability, as our bodies can be if we respect them.

Dr Alexander Lowen, a pioneer in the bioenergy field, established the importance of the connection between the body, especially the lower part (the feet and legs), and the earth to the emotional and psychological aspects of a person. The basic premise is that if we can 'hold our ground' physically then we will feel that we have roots and therefore a place in the world. This connection between earth and body also gives a sense of physical and emotional security which says that you can 'stand on your own two feet'.

I, too, feel its essential value, especially in the field of self-defence/self-preservation. It is difficult to feel our sense of worth unless we feel a connection. This is one reason why so many socially oppressed groups such as women, blacks, children, and older people have increased their awareness of their backgrounds – of their roots. We are re-establishing our worth in the world.

According to Dr Lowen, the saying 'she doesn't have a leg to stand on' is to be taken literally. You cannot transmit feelings *effectively* if you are out of touch with the feelings in your legs and feet. This was a great revelation for me. My grandmother, being of American Indian background, used to tell me as a child that one of the purposes of the native American's dance, which incorporates a lot of stamping into the earth, is to relieve tension and frustration. This all sounded good but I was never quite sure of how it all worked until I began doing some bioenergetic grounding exercises.

American Indians knew the value of connecting with the earth and some of their dances achieved this through stamping.

I had been studying judo, kung fu, aikido, and tai chi along with teaching self-defence and judo for several years. Although I felt confident in physical technique I was searching for a way to be equally strong, confident, and lucid within my emotions and decided to study bioenergetics.

After talking for a while with Alexandra, my teacher, she said 'Now let's look at what your body is saying'. She asked me to stand in a strange position with my feet turned in, my body bent over, with my fingertips touching the ground in front of me. She explained that this was a stressful position designed to charge the body up so that I could feel where the blocks were, or places where I was holding myself back due to old fear, pain, or anger. This was a grounding exercise.

The first thing she noticed was that my feet weren't making solid contact with the ground. 'What do you mean?' I said, surprised, 'my feet are touching the ground.' 'Not entirely,' she replied. 'There are gaps: your heels are off the ground.' She went on to explain how the physical language of my body would translate into an emotional disposition – needing to be on my toes because somewhere, despite all of my martial arts training, I didn't quite trust my ability to take care of myself; not necessarily in a physical confrontation, although this was possible, but more in certain everyday situations.

Even though I didn't like this possibility, I had already accepted that the body doesn't lie. I became aware that I still felt victimized and discriminated against because I am a woman and black – that, despite my fighting this discrimination in my own ways, some of those messages which say 'you can't' had wriggled their way into my belief system. And, as I already mentioned in the resilient arm exercise (page 17), our thoughts are very powerful – what we think has the power to be.

Now I no longer feel that my being a woman or being black will stop me from doing anything I want to do. After having acknowledged the areas where I was a victim, I realized that by continuing to believe I was a victim I would only bring experiences into my life which would continually verify those messages, and so I began to change. This is not, however, to say that women who have been raped or otherwise attacked 'asked for it'.

Working with the body, especially doing grounding exercises, speeds one's realization of ways in which one feels a victim and helps to counter those feelings. So, as women who are working to de-victimize ourselves, and

Explore how it feels to be ungrounded.

be in a position to defend ourselves, we must enter the realm of physical protection by developing a solid foundation through simple grounding exercises.

Let's begin by exploring how it feels to be ungrounded, then go on to grounding. To do the following exercises needs a lot of uninterrupted time – half an hour for the ungrounding one, an hour for a break, then three-quarters of an hour for grounding. If you want to see and feel the beneficial changes any of the exercises that I suggest can bring about, you will need to become accustomed to setting aside the recommended intervals of time. This is doubly important because, by setting aside time for yourself, you are helping to dissolve one harmful root of our conditioning as women – that which says we don't deserve time for ourselves, we should use it to take care of others. This attitude contains a major oversight in that it does not recognize that the more we take care of ourselves, the more we genuinely have to offer others.

To do these exercises you also need a partner. Make sure you choose one who wants to grow as well, not someone who feels threatened.

Ungrounding

1 Imagine that there are a lot of people in the room and that you are concerned about what everyone is thinking of you.

2 Cue your partner to run or walk by, sweeping you off your feet at any time after thirty seconds of your walking around.

3 Reverse roles.

4 Make a hot drink. Sit down and share what it felt like to be in both roles. You might refer to how your bodies felt in each role, how connected or disconnected you felt with the ground, your sense of personal importance, whatever other thoughts were in your mind.

5 Remember the general feeling on both sides.

Allow at least an hour before proceeding to the next exercise as the time lapse will allow you to feel more fully the effect of both parts.

Grounding

1 Stand separately in different parts of the room.

2 Follow the instructions from 2–12; while your partner reads, you follow.

3 Stand with your feet shoulder-width apart and turned inward about forty-five degrees. Bend your knees as close as you can get them to a right angle but don't fret if they will not go this far. Bending from your waist, lower your upper body so that your chest is near your thighs. Reach out and touch the fingertips of both hands to the ground. Gently lower your head and move it from side to side, making sure that your neck is loose.

4 Throughout the remainder of the exercise it is important that every part of your feet touches the ground – heels, soles, toes.

5 Once you have the structure properly set up, you are ready to start moving – building a flow of energy throughout your body. Go over 3 and 4 to ensure that you have followed all the instructions.

6 Now, like a bellows, inhale through your mouth. Fill up your lungs as you bend your knees *very slowly*, letting your feet and legs support the full weight of your body. Keep your fingertips on the ground.

7 *Without fully extending your legs*, exhale (through your mouth) and let some sound out (such as ah! or ha! from your stomach) as you *very slowly* push your hips straight up into the air. The push should come from your feet pushing into the ground rather than from your lifting yourself from your knees or torso. This cannot be stressed enough because *it is through pushing into the earth while your legs are slightly flexed that you begin to feel that deep contact with the earth.* This is the main purpose of this exercise – to establish connection.

8 Repeat the bellows-type rhythm of **6** and **7** at least six times, or until you go one beyond the point where you feel you can do no more (this amount will vary according to how accustomed your body is to being under this type of stress).

9 *As slowly as possible*, begin to push yourself up from your feet, unfolding like a bean sprout, one vertebra at a time (focus your mind on each vertebra). The head should be absolutely the last part to come up.

10 If you experience heat, trembling, or tingling, know that these are all signs of energy being released throughout the body which is a good sign. If you experience pain, be aware of the area because this is where the flow is blocked. Each time that you experience pain in this exercise in the future, use your mind to send your breath gently through that area.

11 To cool down, stand with your feet shoulder-width apart, toes pointed straight ahead this time, knees bent slightly, and breathe. Incorporate, if you like, the feeling of a waterfall, cleansing and strengthening you.

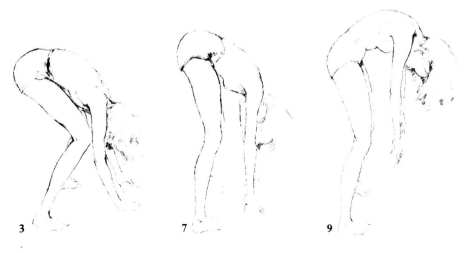

12 When you are ready to imagine yourself stepping from under the water, take a step forward, and sit (crosslegged, or however you are comfortable so long as your bottom and feet are touching the ground) and tune into a quiet place (see page 25), whatever this means to you – in your heart, your mind, your stomach, whatever, as long as it is in your body.

13 Exchange roles and repeat the exercise – reading the instructions for your partner.

14 Next time you go through **3–8**, you may enhance the depth of grounding contact by getting your partner to place their hands and weight on the base of your back. This will give you something tangible to see how much stress your legs can support and thus, will affect your ability to handle stress in a confident manner.

15 Sit down with your partner, have a hot, relaxing drink, and share your experiences. If you feel so moved, write these discussions down in a journal or keep them on tape. It will prove to be quite interesting as you log your progress.

Another key way to establish and build a feeling of being grounded is to learn to do press-ups (see following chapter) and to keep practising them. There is no reason why women should not do press-ups – they are not too hard, this is just one more idea we have been fed in order to reduce our power.

Doing grounding exercises regularly will give strength, vitality, and clarity to your walk and will enhance your circulation – and your ability to spring back in stressful situations. This is why I feel that they are a must for any comprehensive training programme because they encourage and cultivate an internal impulse – an *internal* rather than superimposed response.

14

7
PRESS-UPS FOR WOMEN?

'As women we are born with a natural potential for endurance and strength.'

Just as we need to build the feeling of the support of our legs through grounding, we must also balance that strength through developing the upper part of the body to feel whole. This is especially important for us as women as we are generally not encouraged to develop this area of the body – our arms in particular. This is considered by an awful lot of us to be an exclusively male domain.

Why is this? As we have, over the centuries, been encouraged to take care of others first, plus dealing with the threat of rape which cast us in the role of victims, it is very easy for such suggestions to creep into our minds – unless we have something else in them which leaves no room for these suggestions to breed. Whatever is within our minds gets carried out in our bodies and vice-versa. This happens whether or not we are conscious of it. Since we are told that women are weaker and can't defend themselves this message travels through our collective thoughts as women and manifests itself into a predisposition towards weakness in the upper part of the body.

I used to have this attitude, and to fear that doing press-ups would give me bulging, ugly muscles (which

Press-ups counter the relative weakness in women's upper bodies.

it doesn't). At the same time I had an avid attraction for men with broad shoulders and strong chests. One day, as I was watching such a man, he said, 'You don't even know me – why are you so attracted?' When I told him innocently that it was because of his muscular torso, broad shoulders, and chest, he replied, 'You can have the same strength with a little dedication.' That conversation got me thinking about just what it was that was featured in those qualities that I admired. It was the confidence, the demeanour of strength, the aesthetic clarity in muscular definition, and the feeling of being able to defend oneself. I then realized that I wanted those things for myself, so I began doing *my own style* of press-ups.

I was careful not to do them in an abrupt jerky way because I didn't want to feed my body those qualities. Also, I knew from bioenergetics that practice of this nature, especially around the area of the heart, only leads to building an attitude of armour and defensiveness. I wanted to be able to feel my helplessness and vulnerability from time to time because I had learned that these two qualities, when felt, accepted, and explored, yield greater strength and compassion.

Khaleghl's Press-ups

1 You may do them from your knees and gradually move to doing them from your hands and feet. Warm up generally by circling your shoulders, your elbows, wrists and neck, and get the feeling of supporting yourself by pressing as hard as you can, one hand into the other at the side of your chest. Then do a few press-ups standing up – by pushing your body away from a wall.

1

2 Lie down on your stomach and visualize your whole body being open and full with a current of whatever you like (electricity, water, light, sound).

3 Place your hands, fingers pointing in the direction of your head, directly under each breast. Begin to feel your weight pressing into them – all the way into your fingertips.

3

4 Keep your body long and straight, either from your toes to the top of your head or from your knees to the top. Inhale, filling up the whole of your chest until it pushes down your abdomen.

5 Exhale through your mouth and push yourself up. Feel the full length of your arms in the same way that you did when you practised the resilient arm exercise (page 17). Be conscious of your arms as they support your weight.

6 Inhale again as you go down as far as you can without touching the ground, and exhale as you push up. The breathing is crucial and must be timed with your movement. It keeps your awareness aligned with what is happening inside which minimizes the chances of your putting on a brittle, defensive form of strength. Focusing on your breathing will make your body seem lighter and will supply you with the energy and willpower you need to carry on. It will also encourage resiliency in your arms and chest and back. *Be sure to keep your shoulders down.*

7 If you have never done press-ups before you might want to ask someone to hold your body around the waist, giving you support as you push yourself up and lower yourself. Ask them to hold you until your back, stomach, shoulder, legs, and neck adjust to the structure of press-ups. Maintain a slow, solid rhythm at first. When you can do ten a day with ease, increase your rhythm.

8 If you can do all this and feel quite confident with doing fifty with ease, make sure you are doing them rhythmically and with your breathing correct, then progress to doing press-ups on your fists.

Jumping Up

This exercise further strengthens the heart and gives you stamina, agility and alertness.

1 Start from the press-ups ground position and push yourself up.

2 After you have pushed yourself up, keep your arms extended as they are and, in a jumping and sliding motion, bring your legs between your arms so that you are in a squatting position with your balance on the front half of your feet. Keep your eyes looking straight ahead to the horizon.

3 Now lift your hands and use your arms for balance.

4 Visualize the top of your head reaching up into the sky. Push your feet into the ground and propel yourself into standing.

5 Reverse these instructions and repeat your press-ups. Do one more beyond the point where you feel you are too tired.

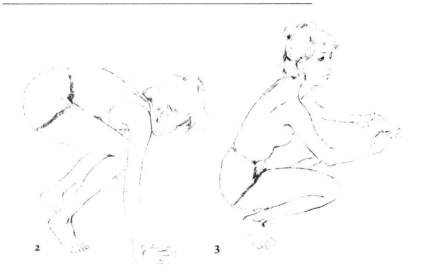

Relaxing the Chest

Another option is to relax your chest completely, letting it become soft as you exhale, lengthening your arms. This exercise will teach you how to relax while you are doing something strenuous and will give you the inner support to do this during stressful times in your daily activities.

You will find that there are times when you feel that you simply cannot do any of these exercises. Besides the fact that you may be tired or hungry, you are probably coming against a mental barrier of 'I can't'. Negative messages have been in there for a while and have developed considerable strength on their own. They are fed by what others have told you and by your own belief system which, by the way, is very tenacious, especially when it has been out of your control, operating passively. These messages, in turn, feed your body's understanding in what it can do. Don't get discouraged because, although these internal messages have gained a lot of strength, they can be persuaded with the truth.

As you try to do press-ups you will probably suffer an internal conflict. New messages of 'I can' and 'I deserve to have' are being intercepted and even seduced by old messages which say 'You can't'. Here is a way to bring everything out into the open and more under your control. This will take fifteen minutes and you need a partner.

Countering the Barrier

1 Think of something that is very important to you. Without concentrating too much, make it into a story such as: 'I would like to be a concert pianist. I realize that it will require lessons, money, and a lot of discipline. Even though it may seem to be a great deal of work I am ready and willing to do it. I will take pleasure from the work and will be able to provide that for others . . .'

2 While you are expressing your chosen story your partner will be sitting about a foot away from your face and will be shaking their head in a 'no' without saying it. They will be denying your every word, but you are to carry on – hold your ground.

3 Tune into how this felt – to carry on, feeling your determination even in the face of adversary.

4 Ask your partner how it felt to deny you.

5 Exchange roles, repeating the exercise. This time the person who is denying will actually say 'No you won't', to your every statement. You will get in touch with your roots as you did in the resilient arm exercise (page 17), and with the sun inside you. Bring it up through your heart, gathering the courage you might need to carry on, and this time tell your story in a more peaceful manner and with even greater conviction.

6 Exchange roles again.

7 Now do a set of your press-ups.
Sometimes getting in touch with our power through our chests and arms brings up feelings of helplessness and anger. Let these come out, and own them: they are landmarks of your strength.

Press-ups help women build purely physical strength in an area where they don't usually have it which, in itself, builds confidence. But, much more, building the upper part of the body has to do with expressing confidence – being able to take from the world what you need and push away what you don't want. Coupled with the effects of grounding, press-ups, done properly, may very well give us back the balance of power and victim-proof consciousness that we so desperately need.

I want to thank the man who was so secure himself that he was able to encourage me in my ability to acquire confidence physically. Also, to a friend of mine who said the world might be different if more women did press-ups; I say, 'I agree!'

To start the Countering the Barrier exercise, think of something important to you and make it into a story.

8
MYTHS AND REALITY

'Questions and doubts come up for all of us when we really begin to feel our sense of power.'

At some point we will have to confront those devilish little voices which say 'All right, so we've worked with self-worth, redefining strength, grounding, press-ups, and talked about intuition. It sounds good and I got something out of those exercises, but what's this really got to do with self-defence – I mean the practical stuff. For instance, what if someone tries to rape me or, worse, if he has a knife, or worst of all, if a gang attacks me, all carrying knives – what am I to do then?'

Have a little patience with yourself. What you have learned so far (if it has been allowed in) is basically enough for you to trust yourself to know what to do – to use your intuition to your advantage. I'd like you to recognize these questions and doubts as natural, as little demons which come up for all of us when we are really beginning to feel our power. You have just touched a deeper layer of conditioning – one whose function can be either to undermine the strength and confidence you have attained so far or to raise some humour, thereby lightening the air a bit so that we can make more progress.

Often these fears have their roots in pervading attitudes and myths about self-defence and rape, so let's expose some of the major ones. We'll start with the classic attitudes held by most people and some self-defence teachers: these keep women from taking steps towards greater self-development and protection.

Myth **Besides it having to do with 'leaving a bloody heap in a blur of speed', learning self-defence will destroy your feminity.**
Response This depends on your definition of feminity. As I see it – how can something whose purpose is greater self-awareness and development destroy femininity unless femininity has to do with depending on someone else for your awareness.

Myth **Learning self-defence will make you into a violent man-hater.**
Response We will be discussing violence later. To give you a preview, though, we all have violence within us. Anyone who has been oppressed or hurt in any way, who has not regained their sense of power in the situation, has a time bomb of rage inside. A proper self-defence class will enable you to look at some of these areas and will provide avenues which will constructively direct this anger and potential violence. If anything, it should make you a more gentle, more creative person.

As for turning you into a man-hater, I have only this to say: no person or event can turn you into anything other than what you want or choose to be. If you hate someone or a group of people, you have your reasons. That is your choice. If you are concerned about being influenced in a self-defence class, ask the teacher and members of the class about their biases; listen, and then decide from there whether or not this is an appropriate learning situation for you.

Myth **If a woman learns self-defence it will only escalate the violence which will be directed towards her.**
Response This reeks of some of that familiar conditioning – we women must stay in our places, otherwise we will be punished.

There is a major difference between fighting and struggling which I will expound in Phase 2. When we looked at how women already defend themselves (page 27), few of those women had studied any self-defence, yet they managed to protect themselves effectively. Some even educated the man without touching him.

Perhaps within this myth the mythmaker is referring

to the consequences of a woman learning physical techniques. In my classes I teach very serious and powerful techniques, many of which are from kung fu, judo, and capoeira (Afro-Brazilian martial art). *All these techniques require very little muscular strength, but rather, use personal judgement, timing, and accuracy as a base.* They are directed to vital parts of the body such as the eyes and groin and thus, are effective in redirecting an attacker's attention back to himself. Women in the classes are encouraged to channel their emotions, as well as their physical strength into this use of their bodies as a weapon. They are especially encouraged to use these weapons as a last resort, and only in moments when they feel that it will be safe for them and to their advantage to do so.

This fear of escalating the man's violence comes, too, from women who have watched a lot of the propaganda which is often implicit in television and cinema films, or from experiences wherein women may have been reluctant to use physical retaliation, but did, and missed a vital part of the attacker's body. This resulted in the attacker becoming angry – a natural response from anybody who has been hit only in a muscular area rather than in a place that really hurts, which would have made them pull all of their attention back into themselves. The problem lies in women not being taught to fight effectively, which is why we see them beating impotently upon men's muscular chests or abdomens rather than going directly for the eyes, or kicking, striking or grabbing up and under into the testicles and groin. This brings us to the next myth.

Myth If women learn self-defence men will have to stay off the streets because women will be so aggressive that they will go around kicking men in the balls indiscriminately.
Response A bit of a corollary to the last one, I encounter this regularly with men and women. It just makes me laugh. I have many more exciting things to share with women regarding the development of their power. Self-defence is an in-depth topic, much more than learning to hurt someone.

Myth If you carry a weapon you don't need self-defence training.
Response To start with, in Britain it is illegal to carry anything that could be called 'an offensive weapon', no matter how much you may have good reason to feel that

you need its protection. You are supposed to avoid violence, running away if possible. If you cannot escape you are supposed to use the minimum force once you have been attacked. If you injure someone when defending yourself, *you* may be prosecuted if the law thinks you over-reacted.

Apart from the legal position, it is essential to realize that you cannot rely on anything (or anyone) other than yourself for your personal care and protection, and so to gain the necessary confidence to take on that responsibility. Keep working through Chapter 4 (page 31) on how to use fear as a source of strength. You can acquire the confidence needed to get through your worst fears by increasing your awareness of your resources – inner and environmental – at all times.

From a practical point of view, anything you carry can be taken from you and used against you, especially a

In Britain, it is illegal to carry anything that could be called 'an offensive weapon', even a pair of scissors.

knife or gun. Also, any 'weapon' – even if it were something that it could be claimed was necessary and normal to have on you, such as your keys or a heavy torch – would have to be carried immediately to hand to be of any use, and this is rarely convenient.

Far better protection is provided by bearing in mind that you live with a potential arsenal of ready-to-use weapons that cannot be wrested from you – your feet and hands used in various ways, even your head. We will explore our bodies as weapons in Phase 2. As self-defence relies on responding to anything that may endanger you in such a way that you retain power, in an emergency you might consider looking swiftly around you to see what could be turned into a weapon – a stone or fallen branch, a chair, cushion, or glass of water. However, again you might fall foul of the law which, in Britain, is very strict about how much force you may use to defend yourself (see page 5).

Myth **If an attacker has a weapon then anything which you have learned in self-defence classes won't apply.**
Response Again, not if you trust your intuition and have a knowledge of how and where to use your body weapons (Phase 2), both generally and specifically when someone is armed (page 136).

Myth **Training in a martial art provides an adequate self-defence.**
Response Receiving my black belt in judo did not make me feel that I could defend myself. The confidence came when I began to get grounded – when I realized that I have a reason and a right to be alive – in combination with my building on the credit of the frequently unspectacular ways that I had diverted aggression.

Unless there is specific guidance directed towards increasing people's sense of worth interspersed with technique, a martial art does not provide adequate self-defence. In fact, unless it is taught in such a way to inspire students' creativity, it might be a hindrance because students may be locked into a rigid attack-defend pattern which they cannot adapt for different contingencies. I do, however, feel that a martial arts training facilitates quicker reflexes, greater mind-body-spirit co-ordination, grace, and a peaceful disposition. This is also true of other strenuous physical disciplines including dance, yoga, tennis, squash, badminton, gymnastics, running and team sports such as netball.

9
THE ATTACKER WITHIN

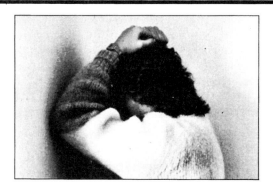

> *'Each of us has our own ways of attacking ourselves, don't we?'*

'Why didn't you do it better?' 'You should get something done.' 'You'll never be any good at it.' Have you ever said any of these things to yourself? If your answer is yes to at least two of them, you had better learn to defend yourself from yourself because the chances are that you have a pretty vicious attacker inside.

When we berate ourselves with phrases such as the above, or when we absorb other ones which might have been said to us down through the years (or in the case of a particular culture or race, down through the ages), we each become our worst enemy. To get more of a tangible grip on this concept through your body try this exercise:

Beating Yourself Down

1 Stand in the middle of a room.

2 Hit yourself repeatedly as hard as you feel is safe, in different places. Stop when you feel tired, then immediately close your eyes, Be aware of the sensation in your body.

3 In which direction do you feel it moving (in, out, circular)?

4 Now get in touch with a quiet place within (page 25).

5 Use your mind and will as you did in the resilient arm exercise (page 17) and attempt to direct the power of your roots and your internal sun *out* through your body in all directions.

If you find difficulty in doing 5, which is often the case, you are beginning to see and feel the effects that guilt, negativity, and a low sense of self-worth have on your willpower, on your ability to direct your power outward – your ability to 'communicate the value of your life'. Beating yourself down with messages such as the above is not very different from an external attacker beating upon you. These messages very insiduously break down confidence, courage, your ability to give and receive love, and your ability to express yourself creatively. These messages, or internal attackers, drain all your faculties. They block your ability to contact your natural protective resources, such as health, confidence, will, physical/mental/emotional strength and stamina, and righteous anger.

Perhaps you were beaten, emotionally or physically, as a child, adolescent, wife, lover, or otherwise and some of those messages are still lingering. Let me assure you that if I appear to be casual in my approach to this matter, this is only because of my respect for the individual and my faith in our personal and collective abilities to change these wretched experiences into sources of strength. I do know of and empathize with how damaging these experiences can be. All of us have been bruised in some form, some more severely than others.

However, although I do believe that we can overcome even the most severe damage in time, we can speed up this process in a very gentle way – one which I call the pebble in the lake feeling. The concept is that, through acknowledging one simple way that you attack yourself (without judgement), you can effectively ripple love and radiance into areas of self-hatred which are even more severe and some of which are, perhaps, unconscious – without ever having to dredge up the details. Once this pebble of love and radiance has been cast into the lake of self-hatred, it continues to ripple out until it has turned all the hatred back into a lake of self-love. Once it has been restored, its magnificent radiance will allow no room for messages of attack.

To help you start that pebble of self-love, here is my adapted version of an exercise from a therapy called transactional analysis. Reserve a whole morning or afternoon, free of interruptions, as it will take three to five hours to do this one justice. You may experience it alone or with another person, but make sure it's someone that you feel close to.

Creating a Nurturing Guide

You will need:
- a place which is warm and has a bath and a bed or beds, plus facilities for playing your favourite music
- something warm to drink
- paper without lines – preferably large pieces
- coloured crayons
- a blanket for each person doing the exercise

1 To prepare:

a put the paper and crayons in the room in which you feel most comfortable

b put on some of your favourite soothing music or any which inspires you

c make yourself a cup of your favourite hot drink

d make sure the blanket and bed are ready

e do Part 2 of the grounding exercise (page 42) and three press-ups (page 46)

2 Now you are ready to begin. Go into the room with the paper and crayons and music.

3 Choose your favourite colour from the crayons.

4 Let yourself be a child again and recall, if you will, what it would be like to have an ideal nurturing guide – someone or something you could go to even when you have done the worst thing you can imagine and still get only support, wisdom, and guidance.

5 Now place the crayon in the hand that you do not normally write with. This is to prevent you writing something down too quickly, taking its meaning for granted. You need to feel what you are writing.

Have everything you need to hand before beginning the Nurturing Guide exercise.

6 Using very simple language – that of a young child – describe in words, or pictures, or both, your nurturing guide – one which you have created. If you happen to know someone who has been in that role for you, you may describe their qualities.

7 Take another sheet of paper and, again using the hand you do not normally write with, write down the type of things this guide says that makes them so comforting – that makes you feel safe, giving you the strength to carry on, growing and blossoming with each encounter.

8 Keeping in touch with the feeling, read both pages silently to yourself.

9 Now read them aloud to yourself, still keeping connected with your feelings. Stay with your guide for at least ten minutes, and when you are ready go into the bathroom and run a warm bath. If you feel tearful (when I do this exercise I always cry at some point during the day) let yourself cry with joy or in the releasing of sadness or whatever. Crying is an essential part of this exercise as it is a natural thing to do when you are letting go of an old part that may have once served you – even old feelings of self-doubt and guilt.

10 As the bath is running put your guide up on a clearly visible and well-lit wall to remind you of the guide which is within you when 'I should' and 'Why didn't you try' try to creep in. Begin to replace those messages with 'I did', 'I will' and 'I won't'.

11 Take a nice warm bath and lavish yourself in love.

12 Wrap yourself in your blanket and take a nap. When you wake up drink lots of fluid.

13 Next, do the grounding exercise (page 42).

14 Carry on with your normal activities for the rest of the day. After this exercise you will probably feel very drained, especially if you cried a lot, but you should also feel a deep sense of calm and peace.

If you can go and have a massage within a few days of doing this exercise, do so. Feel each stroke as pouring love into yourself – love which you deserve. As this love pebble gently releases its waves into deeper barriers of self-doubt and hatred, you may feel like crying, laughing, or just having a physical or creative release. Don't worry; this is old skin sloughing off. It no longer fits.

10
INTRODUCING THE ELEMENTS

'The more you can identify with the elements, the more you can directly tap their power.'

Through analysing and studying the qualities of the elements of earth, water, fire and air, we can appropriate their power and complexity for our own use in helping us to defend ourselves. By keeping in mind the qualities of the relevant element or elements when practising the physical self-defence techniques in Phase 2, the techniques can be made more alive, and more effective.

Some of the primary *earth element* aspects of self-preservation have already been discussed in Phase 1 – such as grounding (Chapter 6) and confronting fear and transforming it (Chapter 4).

The parts and functions of the body which actually supply the base and resource of knowledge for your strength and ability to protect yourself physically are related to earth. This resource of knowledge, when developed, will enable you to draw on the necessary materials, people and aspects of the environment to enhance your mental and physical development. It will also create confidence which will act as a cushion, protecting you from things, people and forces which could interfere with your development.

The earth element is involved in the physical understanding and action of all self-preservation. Specifically, it includes being at ease with physical contact (Phase 1, Chapter 5), strengthening exercises (Phase 1, Chapter 7; Phase 2, Chapter 1), knowledge of vulnerable target areas of the body (page 78), knowing your impact when punching (page 125), use of your voice (page 84), evading being held with minimum effort (Phase 2, Chapter 3), and knowing how to use your body as a weapon (page 80 and Phase 2, Chapters 6, 7 and 8).

The *water element* techniques of self-defence include acknowledgement of personal emotional patterns, feelings, ways of blending with an attacker (page 92), escapes from grips, pins or sticky situations (Phase 2, Chapter 4), and ways of falling or blending safely with the ground (Phase 2, Chapter 5).

The techniques related to the *fire element* include being able to feel and direct your anger (page 123) and kicking (Phase 2, Chapter 6). Fire can be used as a resource of protection (Phase 2, Chapter 3), and of unpredictable and unique responses to situations. It has relevance to activities with others which enhance your feelings of self-worth (Phase 1, Chapter 2).

The *air element* techniques include use of intuition (Phase 1, Chapter 2 and Phase 3), using fear as a source of strength (Phase 1, Chapter 4), and throwing techniques (Phase 2, Chapter 8).

Some of you may find yourselves gravitating by preference to one or two of these elements. This is natural and due, in part, to the fact that each of us feels basically comfortable with one particular element and the qualities which relate to it. Once you have identified the element that you are most at home with and worked on its techniques, building up techniques which relate to the other elements will produce a balance and can have a lot of benefits. For instance, if you are an earth person, doing the water techniques outlined above may boost your energy level and confidence.

There are many possibilities of dynamic combinations between the elements which you may play with in your own time. Certain of these elements will attract you at different times.

Emotional Bondage

By making links between the elements and certain emotions, we can take a shortcut to breaking out of emotional bondage. Sometimes, when we start to feel an emotion, it takes us over. By translating your emotions into different qualities of energy, you can break free of the possibility of being paralysed by them. Expressing anger and fear are important things to do, provided that you can move on to having a feeling of balance. If, however, you find that after you have expressed the emotion, you cannot regain your sense of well-being, try mentally translating the emotion into one of the elements: you can utilize an intermediate emotion, too. For instance, change fear into anger, then the anger into fire. This will give you the energy to make the necessary decisions about what to do about the situation that caused your original emotion, and for you to take action.

These are some other ways of breaking free from emotions which are trapping you. Change:
- anger into fire
- sadness into water
- love into fire and water
- excitement into fire and water
- fear into anger into fire
- depression into sadness into anger into fire
- frustration into earth into fire

When you have freed yourself from the hold of the emotion and translated its intensity into energy, ask yourself how does that particular element function in nature and this will give you insight into the use you can make of its qualities in your life, releasing you from psychological and emotional bondage, which often expresses itself in the words 'I can't'.

Once you are proficient at transmuting an emotion to an element and breaking out of your initial emotional bondage, you can go on to think yourself from one element into another. This helps even more to restore your balance and enables you to channel your energy into something constructive.

Getting to Know the Elements

To get really close to the spirit of each element, read and think about the specific qualities of each one and work at mentally becoming it, as in these simple exercises. All the elements are necessary for a sense of balance and harmony, so don't neglect any of them. The more you can identify with the elements, the more you can directly tap their powers. The result will be a repertoire of originally strong self-defence techniques, a feeling of strength and harmony, and a greater connection with nature and all that is related to it.

Earth

1 What are its qualities?
- solid
- steady
- heavy
- firm
- supportive
- add any other qualities that occur to you

The earth provides the base for growth. The fruit, tree or flower which is produced is a reflection both of the quality of the seed and of the quality of nourishment it receives along its way to development.

2 Stand with the feet shoulder-width apart. Ensure they are making full contact with the ground and that your weight is distributed evenly over every part of them.

3 Now review the earth qualities in 1 by saying them aloud as you stand in this position. Feel these qualities in your mind, and then let them filter systematically down your body, permeating all your muscles, into your feet.

4 Maintain this feeling for one minute. It is very important that you *become* the earth, rather than creating a separation through pretending. Saturate yourself (mind, body, spirit) with these qualities, and revel in them (smell and feel the earth).

Water

1 What are its qualities?
- fluid
- soft
- sensual
- powerful
- flows to the lowest point
- cannot be grasped
- takes on the shape of its container
- add any other qualities that occur to you

As water is a softer, more fluid, element than earth, it bears the ability to soften hardness.

2 As in the earth exercise, feel all these qualities in your body and try to become water.

3 Maintain this feeling for one minute.

Water softens earth and absorbs shock, so it may be used as a primary quality in practising feinting to remove your target areas from an attacker (page 81). Similarly, you may use the qualities of water to avoid injury and to blend with the earth when practising falls (page 109).

It is also an element of reflection and thus deals with feeling which provides a link between thought and action. Water plays a very important part in our lives. It covers two-thirds of our world, and our human bodies are ninety per cent fluid. This suggests that a high proportion of our being is feeling and we are, therefore, susceptible to the pull of our feelings. There is a constant feedback between our feelings and the mind.

Water can run deep beneath the surface and, when unacknowledged and unchannelled, can eventually undermine solid structures. This is why it is to our advantage to understand as much as we can the motivation for our actions. One way to do this is to remember and pay attention to your dreams; another is to see if there are patterns within your moods over a time of, say, a month. It will be useful for you to acknowledge the way you feel before you deal with other people, rather than have someone take advantage of a blind spot.

Fire

1 What are its qualities?
- hot
- unpredictable
- enticing
- spontaneous
- gives warmth
- add any other qualities that occur to you

2 As in the earth exercise, feel all these qualities in your body and try to become fire.

3 Maintain this feeling for one minute.

As fire has to do with spontaneous creative expression, the uses of this element include spontaneous expression of all the physical techniques I mention. This element has to do with *dancing* these techniques – whereas earth serves to build the technique solidly into the body and water has to do with flowing and absorbing.

Just as dance is composed of different rhythms, this is true of the expression of fire through the techniques. Fire can be alternately fast and slow, long and drawn out, or concentrated and blasting. All of these rhythms can manifest themselves in a matter of seconds. It is the element which pulls all of the others together and allows you to express yourself creatively within the moment.

Fire activities include anything that inspires creativity, anything that gets the heart pumping faster than usual, such as aerobic exercises, brisk walking, running, dancing, etc. You may strengthen the fire within you by participating in one of these activities.

The fire element also has to do with expressing anger and kicking swiftly (page 116).

Air

1 What are its qualities?
- light
- invisible
- nowhere and everywhere
- elusive
- cannot be grasped
- difficult to contain
- add any other qualities that occur to you

The most elusive of all the elements, air is everywhere, connecting all living, breathing organisms.

2 As in the earth exercise, feel all these qualities in your body and try to become air.

3 Maintain this feeling for one minute.

The techniques involving air include methods of throwing (page 130); and communications, through speech, thought and intuition (page 20). Just as animals and insects detect change in the weather by the air, so we can detect changes in people's thoughts and in our environment by opening ourselves to the air element within us.

Harmonizing the Elements

The natural state of the different elements is harmony with each other. Look at the earth, the ocean, the sun and the air. See and feel how they work together. Once you open yourself to an understanding of the elements and the part they play in your life you will be able to draw on their qualities as a resource. Anyone who then attacks you will find themselves dealing with the strength of a tree, or a wave, or the sun, or a cloud. This will totally disconcert them, make them off-balance, and give you a lot of additional power in defending yourself. By cultivating the quiet place inside yourself (see page 25), you can create room within you, within your perspective, for the different elements to live.

PHASE 2
TECHNIQUE

'Learning to punch and kick effectively means you develop confidence in your physical abilities.'

1

AGILITY AND STAMINA

*'You must be prepared –
psychologically and physically – to
stumble, fall and get up from there.'*

We learnt in Phase 1 the importance of using self-worth as an impulse for fighting and developing comfort with physical contact. It is equally important that you develop basic agility for protecting and preserving yourself. As we have seen, leaving 'a bloody heap in a blur of speed' does not characterize the essential realm of self-defence. You *may* have to fall down, stand up, roll over, sit up, roll backwards, jump up, stamp down, push yourself up, or any combination of the above, in the course of protecting yourself physically; and you may have to perform these manoeuvres mentally in everyday life.

Often, as we grow to be adults, striving for our identity in the world, dealing with the daily challenges, it is easy to forget the physical and mental agility we once had as children. It is easy to forget how it felt to really want something, and to be willing to crawl and stumble, fall and get up again, over and over until, finally, after so much practice, the parts integrate, and the desire is fulfilled. Remember yourself as a child – how it felt to really want to learn to walk or ride a bicycle or swim. Did it all happen overnight? How much were you willing to do to achieve each skill?

As adults we may have raised our expectations of ourselves so much that we lose patience with an organic learning process, which takes time, and adaptability and a willingness to change. This results in our dropping out of a class when we can't do something perfectly straight off. The humility and patience we once had as children has gone. Our dreams evaporate into frustration, possibilities minimize.

So, it is true in actual physical fighting you must be prepared and willing to stumble, fall and get up from there. If this disposition is not cultivated within your attitude and, consequently, your body, you are most likely to be overcome by the possibility of fighting. That doesn't mean you should engage in a physical fight just because you feel insulted: walking or running away from danger is also a way of fighting for what you want. However, by maintaining a basic level of agility in your body, you can preclude possible confrontations and use your energy towards fulfilling more of your life goals and dreams.

Although muscular flexibility enhances agility, it is not the key factor. What is essential is the *mental* ability to move around an oncoming force quickly so it doesn't reach the stage of immobilizing you. Both stamina and strength, together with the willingness to change positions quickly, are necessary for preserving a basic level of agility. Here is an exercise I learned in an anti-violence workshop, which I find useful for this. Do it with a partner; you will need a clock or watch with a second hand.

Developing Agility and Stamina

1 Partner orders you to do the following movements for thirty seconds. Their voice should be loud and slightly abrasive, as this will simulate an edge of pressure, which is within a fighting situation.

Stand up, sit down, roll over, stand up, jump up, run in a circle three times, fall down, roll forward, sit up, squat, stand up, then run four figures-of-eight.

2 Switch positions, as agility also refers to the ability to give clear orders and make quick decisions.

3 The next time you do this increase the time by fifteen seconds, then to a minute.

4 Ideally, this should be done every day, but take your time; build up to this slowly. Start off twice a week, then three times, and so on.

Keeping up an activity such as swimming will give you agility and stamina.

You will notice a change in your approach to challenge immediately. In order for this disposition to last and become a natural part of you, it must be done regularly for at least nine months. If you already do activities which require quick change and stamina, such as swimming, gymnastics, tennis, begin to realize that you have been building potential fighting skills through regular practice of them.

Here is an exercise routine for general conditioning which will provide a sense of well-being. It takes only fifteen minutes, during which time, be sure to keep breathing evenly. You will need a clock or watch with a second hand.

Well-being Programme

1 Grounding (page 42).
a Do exercise until the change in the body becomes evident (trembling in legs).
b Hold for thirty seconds.
c Slowly unwind (taking thirty seconds to one minute), one vertebra at a time. The head should remain loose from the neck until the very end: it is the last thing to come up.

2 Calf stretches, in preparation for knee bends.
a Lean with hands on a wall.
b Placing one leg back from the other, bend front knee to just over the toe.
c Extend back heel into the ground slowly and rhythmically.
d Switch legs and repeat.
e Repeat each pair of stretches six times.

3 Holding knee bends. This will strengthen the entire buttocks and legs and joints of the leg and increase balance.
a Stand with feet shoulder-width apart, toes pointing straight ahead.
b Bring your arms behind you and tightly hold your left wrist with your right hand.
c Lift your heels as high as you can, so that your weight is being supported entirely on the balls of your feet.
d Bend your knees so that your thighs are as close, and parallel, to the ground as possible.
e Hold this position for thirty seconds.
f Repeat. This time the left hand tightly grips the right wrist. Complete the rest of the exercise and hold for thirty seconds.

4 Deep knee bends. These strengthen agility for up and down motions.
a Keep your back straight, with hands on your hips and feet turned out forty-five degrees.
b Lift your heels.
c Keeping your knees pointed out over your toes, go straight down as deep as you can, keeping your back straight and neck long.

d Push yourself up from the balls of your feet, and feel the length of your legs and torso.

e Drop your heels. Feel the length of your body, and the weight of your body balanced evenly on both feet. Repeat ten times.

5 Lower back presses into the ground, for lower back toning.

a Lie on your back and bring your feet close to your hips.

b Press your lower back into the ground by tilting your pelvis upwards.

c Release your lower back muscles by allowing the pelvis to rock back where it was. Repeat ten times.

6 Half sit-ups, to strengthen abdominal muscles and lower back.

a Position yourself as in **5**.

b Hands clasped behind your head, lift your shoulders about thirty degrees from the ground and hold that position for three counts.

c When your shoulders are up, make sure you protect your lower back by pressing it into the ground as in **5**. Repeat ten times. If this is easy, double the repetitions.

7 Knees in with chest. Lie on your back with hands clasped behind your head. Bring your knees into your chest, then extend your legs long by pointing your toes. Keep your feet about 15 cm (6 in) from the ground, until you have done this ten times.

8 Loosen shoulders, elbows, wrists and neck, as explained in preparation for press-ups (page 46).

9 Press-ups for pectoral strengthening. Do five to twenty; you may break them into sets of five.

10 Stand on your hands for pectoral and whole upper body strengthening. Balance against a wall and push through your arms as though they were your legs supporting your full weight.

10

11 Physical illumination.

a Stand up with your feet on the ground, with your toes slightly bent.

b Face a source of light (preferably the sun, moon or a candle flame).

c Feel the strength in your hips, back strong and straight, neck long (make sure your head can float freely from side to side). Feel your body stretched, your feet solid on the ground and your head floating in the

heavens. Keep your arms extended downward with fingers pulled in slightly (the feeling is that they are dipping into the well of your soul, into the resources in life).
d Your head is in contact with your special star.
e Shower yourself with gold light.
f Over this, add a circle of white light.

If you follow this programme, in combination with eating a really good, nutritionally balanced diet, and tuning into the quiet place (page 25), you will feel a solid foundation of balance for performing any self-defence techniques, and in your life generally.

2
USING YOUR BODY WEAPONS

'When it comes to using your weapons, remember, you did not start the violence – you are being attacked.'

Knowing that you have the physical means to back up your sense of worth will give you a solid foundation of confidence. Your body becomes a resource of all the ammunition you need to protect and preserve yourself. You need not rely upon any 'offensive weapon' or an accompanying man to accomplish this. Once you know that you have the ability to redirect someone's harmful attention from you back to them by pressing their eyes into their brains, temporarily paralysing them with a sharp kick or blow up and under into the groin, or by making them dance like a puppet with the threat of breaking their little finger, your body takes on a different disposition – one which projects these abilities.

Hopefully, by the mere virtue of your knowledge of these weapons, you will be able to avoid danger. These techniques are serious and should be exercised with good judgement. However, should the occasion arise when you are in a life-death situation, you will have the tools you need to fight. In any case, knowing them will give you the edge of confidence that will ward off some insecure person who is looking for a helpless victim. The following true story, although possibly an over-reaction to the situation, is an example of this fact.

One day one of my students was sun bathing on the beach. The people on the beach were spread out at some distance from one another so there was plenty of room. A man approached Janet and sat down very close to her without asking if this was all right. Janet felt intruded on and asked him to leave. He was drunk and replied, 'Yeah . . . yeah . . .' but didn't move. Once again she demanded that he leave. He didn't. Then she began to get angry and thought, 'I've always wondered how it would feel to use some of these techniques I've learned in my self-defence class. What would it feel like if I used the heel of my hand to push under his chin?'

As soon as she seriously considered doing this, he scampered off. She didn't even have to touch him, and, although I would naturally never recommend anybody to initiate such action in a situation like this, he must have felt the potential.

I believe that if all women had a physical connection with their physical fighting ability, the possibility of attack and rape would be dramatically reduced.

The Major Body Weapons

The bulk of techniques that I will refer to come from kung fu, others are from judo, and capoeira (Afro-Brazilian martial art dance). Common to all of these techniques is their origin in the spirits of different animals, such as the tiger, cobra, monkey, crane and bear, and in levers, or useful movements in our daily lives which require the least amount of effort to elicit the greatest effect, such as in the use of a hammer or a can opener.

As a result, these techniques are powerful, ranging in their potential to disorient, temporarily paralyse, cause damage to muscles, joints and major organs, to cause unconsciousness or even death, depending upon the intention of the force behind them. **That is why they must be executed only in the context of self-defence, and as a last resort when *you feel* your body, life, or someone or something that is precious to you is in danger.**

Target Areas

I'm sure many of you have seen the repeated weak and derogatory images of women on cinema and TV films and in advertisements, especially the image of women pounding aimlessly on a man's chest while he stands there smugly holding her. Had she known that her body is a potential weapon in combination with the fact that he has vulnerable areas, there would have been a different story. Had she used the heel of her hand under his chin with the alacrity of a rocket, he wouldn't be standing there looking so smug!

We each have areas in and on our bodies which are vulnerable to minimum pressure, some more than others. It is important to know these, so that we can go for them on an attacker if we need to, and also so that we can protect them on ourselves.

Just as it saves time and energy to have a map when you are in strange territory, so it is true of having a map of the vulnerable parts of the body (page 78) as this knowledge can reduce a hulk of an attacker to a human being with vulnerabilities. No matter how much muscle he has, if he has eyes and a groin, he is vulnerable to you.

These areas have been called vital points, and nerve centres. They respond in different ways to different intentions. You may gently rub the temples to relieve pressure, but a sharper blow with different intention could be fatal. It is important, too, that we know these vital points precisely so that we don't waste time and energy striking an area where we will have no effect. Although there are many of these areas, some subtle, some more obvious, the basic ones are more than adequate as a repertoire, and require little time to remember. When you come to study the list of major body weapons and the drawings of suggested target areas for their use, touch these target areas on yourself, feel how it would feel to be hit with the various body weapons you are developing.

When using your weapons, present only half your body to the target.

Key Points in Practising

- Establish a solid base.

a Keep both feet on the ground. Keep your weight low.

b Maintain double your shoulder-width in distance between your feet.

c Bend the front knee to the point where when you look down, you cannot see your foot, and no more nor less than that. If you have to move with the target, maintain the distance between your feet.

d Remember your connection with the earth, as in the grounding exercises (page 42). Let your weight drop down into your legs.

- Present only half of your body to the target. If you do a kick or punch with your body square to someone, they can do the same back to you. By emanating the technique from half of your body, you cut the amount of your body that you need to protect in half.

- Keep your body relaxed and reserve strength for the point of contact.

- Take on the spirit underlying the technique. Just as you become any of the elements in order to receive their power (see page 60), so should you *become* the animal or tool that you are embodying – become a cobra, or a tiger.

Using Your Weapons

On pages 78–80 are the key body weapons that you carry with you at all times, together with a range of some of the vulnerable parts of the body where they can be used. Study them well.

I am assuming that, if you are serious about the whole subject of self-defence, you will want to attend some type of martial arts class – judo, karate, or whatever you choose – (see page 161) – as this will ensure that you are involved in a constant process of learning and growth. It will certainly be necessary for you to be taught face to face in order really to understand and become proficient in using your body weapons and directing them effectively to suitable targets.

Carefully observe the principles behind the movements listed in How to Use Your Weapons (page 80) and what you are taught in classes and, through repeated practice, they will become stronger and more reliable resources for you. When you have mastered the movements, I recommend setting aside at least two hours at a time, as often as you can, to practise everything ten times using one side of the body, and ten times using the other – it is important that strength, agility and co-ordination should be developed equally on both sides of the body. Do this rhythmically. If you have a metronome, set it at different speeds, building up from largo: this will focus your practice and give a precise and crisp quality to your movements.

So that you can make a start now, some of the techniques are demonstrated in the remainder of Phase 2. Some of them are very simple and you will be able to grasp their use from the photographs in this section.

Where to Strike

The 'maps' of potential target areas shown on these pages serve to provide a visual reference list of where to strike. Below each area of the body annotated we have suggested appropriate body weapons.

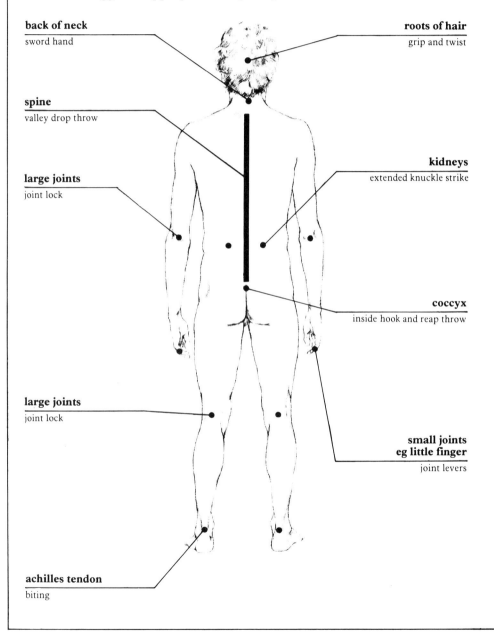

back of neck
sword hand

spine
valley drop throw

large joints
joint lock

large joints
joint lock

achilles tendon
biting

roots of hair
grip and twist

kidneys
extended knuckle strike

coccyx
inside hook and reap throw

small joints eg little finger
joint levers

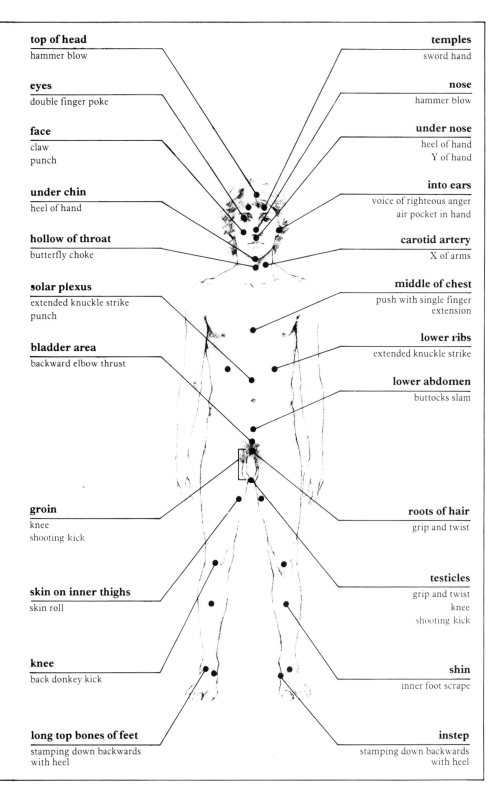

How to use your Weapons

hammer blow
symbol: hammer

butterfly choke
symbol: pincers

back donkey kick
symbol: donkey

push with single finger extension
symbol: teacher's pointer

inner foot scrape
symbol: paint scraper

grip and twist
symbols: boa constrictor, small bottle lid being screwed tightly

extended knuckle strike
symbol: spear

stamping down backwards with heel
symbol: driving stake into ground

double finger poke
symbol: cobra

backward elbow thrust
symbol: big stick striking gong

biting
symbol: steel gin trap

sword hand
symbols: sickle, sabre

knee
symbol: steel pendulum moving at speed of a click

inside hook and reap throw
symbol: scythe

heel of hand
symbol: rocket

valley drop throw
symbol: slice and wrap

voice of righteous anger
symbol: lion's roar

shooting kick
symbol: cannon

air pocket in hand
symbol: teacup

skin roll
symbols: bee sting, snap of fingers

joint locks
symbol: breaking sticks over knee

joint levers
symbol: centrifuge

buttocks slam
symbol: swinging long sandbag

claw
symbol: tiger

punch
symbol: spear

X of arms
symbol: steel cross

Y of hand
symbol: water divining stick

Don't be Squeamish

Many women find the thought of actually executing techniques to the testicles and eyes repulsive. One women said, 'I thought you'd have to be a monster to kick a man in the groin. I never thought of the context of what he might be doing to me.' This is because of the conditioning women undergo to take care of others at all costs, even though they may be attacking you. In order to counter this conditioning, it is important to keep clear *why* you are striking someone.

Also, I have heard many self-defence teachers say you shouldn't go for the groin because men are now aware that women are studying self-defence and that's the first area they'll go to protect. Besides, they say, this action will only anger them.

Most of these teachers have been men, so I can somewhat understand why they'd say this. Whether or not a man who is attacking you is holding that area makes little difference, if you are accurate in going up and under (page 121). What is important, though, is your timing and physical positioning in relation to this. In other words, you should stay out of the range of his arms. You should either be close enough to use your knee or far enough out of the range of a possible punch that you can use a kick from a solid base. If you are accurate, he may be angry twenty minutes later, when he can stand up again. Hopefully, you won't be waiting around for him.

Although the testicles and the eyes are the most foolproof of the vulnerable parts of the body to strike, it is advisable always to go direct to the one which is most available, rather than putting yourself at a disadvantage by reaching for an area that is more remote.

Feinting

One thing you can do if someone strikes out at you is to utilize their intention of inflicting pain on you by acting up. Have you noticed how the head and hands always go towards the area in pain immediately after it happens? If you hurt your knee, your head moves in that direction. If you are hit in the stomach, your head and hands move there.

When you feel you are about to be hit in one of your vulnerable parts you can pre-empt it happening by anticipating the pain and identifying with it before you experience it. Step back, bending your body, as if you have already been struck. This will prevent you receiving the full blow and will hold the attacker's aggression momentarily as they will think they have already succeeded in defeating you. Once you remove your target area, you set up a vacuum which can be used to pull the person off-balance, and into your area of advantage. Then you can proceed from there with a follow-through technique (page 91).

It is instinctive for someone's head and hands to go towards the area of pain – say their knee or stomach – when they are hit.

Achieving Accuracy

When you strike any of the target areas, you want the result to be that the attacker redirects his attention from you to himself in response to the pain he feels. To ensure this, accuracy is extremely important: *always look* before you strike, but always with a quick, covert glance so your attacker isn't made aware from the direction of your focus where you intend to strike. Looking will channel the force of your blow to achieve the greatest intensity. It also stops you hitting someone quite innocent!

When you move, do so swiftly, cleanly and compactly, coming neatly back to a balanced position. This is the most efficient way of delivering a blow, enables you to retain your balance, and avoids giving any preliminary indication of what you are about to do – such as by waving your whole arm around. As well as being accurate, you need to study how to strike or you will lose the advantage of having picked the right target.

The Stationary Target

1 This exercise needs a partner. Stand with your feet shoulder-width apart. Take a lunging step, using your little finger and extending from your centre, and repeatedly point to a target area on your partner's body. The purpose of using the little finger is to ensure accuracy. It is easy to guess at a target area; then you may miss, which will only anger your attacker. Through conscientious practice, you will become accurate.

2 Before you move on to the next target area, come back to the centre of your body.

The Moving Target

This exercise will enable you to get the timing of a strike accurate. Suspend a small ball from a ceiling by a piece of strong string. Get it moving and practise striking it, first with your little finger and then with your body weapons.

Having Impact

The following exercise will show you how to give power and impact to the techniques you execute.

Punching Pillows

1 Have your partner hold the pillow in front of their abdomen.

2 Make a fist with your thumb uppermost (page 124). Tense your body and punch into the pillow. How far did you move your partner?

3 Now relax your shoulders and swing your whole torso and punch your partner (page 125). Was there any difference in the distance they moved?

4 Now exhale and repeat the punch. Was there any difference?

5 Now think of striking *through* your partner rather than at the target.

You should find that a relaxed technique with a solid base is much more powerful and productive than one which is tense: when you breathe and project through and beyond the target you have much more impact.

The Power of Your Voice

Much of how we project ourselves in the world comes through our voice. If your voice is weak, high-pitched and expressed from the back of your mouth, your effect on people will be minimal, and possibly irritating. To project true confidence, which comes from feeling that you have a purpose in life, the voice must start from the feet and legs as a base of support, rumble through the stomach, heart and chest region, and project from the well of the throat. Through regular practice of the following exercise, you can strengthen and tune your voice, which will result in your natural gain of confidence.

Unearthing Your Voice's Power

Stay with each sound you make until it literally vibrates throughout the indicated parts of your body. Repetition of this exercise should yield a greater volume from all the sounds each time.

1 Stand with your feet solidly on the ground – think of the earth (page 63).

2 Place your hands on your stomach and let out the sound 'o' for as long as you can with one breath. The sound should come from your stomach.

3 Now place your hands on your diaphragm area (the horizontal line just below the ribs) and with a full breath, let out the sound 'ah'.

4 Now place your right index finger on the centre of your breastbone and let the sound 'ah' resonate throughout your chest.

5 Placing your hand over your throat, let this area express the sound of 'i'.

6 Now, with your fingertips on the centre of your forehead, let out the sound 'e'. Use your feet as support and squeeze the muscles in your legs and buttocks to give strength to this sound.

7 Finally, place your left hand on your stomach, a little below your navel, and your right hand on the crown of your head, and express the sound 'oi'.

8 Then go back to your stomach with the sound 'o' for grounding.

Regular practice of this exercise (at least once a week) will strengthen the quality of your voice so that your communication will be clearer and will have greater impact. Your 'yeses' and 'nos' will be stronger, as you will be in yourself. When you have worked on your voice in this way, then practise really shouting. Making a great noise when you are attacked has three values.

- It shocks the attacker and instils fear in him.
- It concentrates the power of any strike that you deliver to defend yourself.
- It may be heard by other people, drawing attention to your attacker and discomforting him.

You can direct your voice specifically into one of your attacker's ears (page 80), even damaging the eardrum. Or just lunging forward in an attacking attitude, shouting fiercely, can be effective in scaring him off, so practise this. Then do it when you are practising kicks (page 116), upper body strikes (page 122) and throws (page 130), timing your shouts to correspond with the impact of your blows or the point where you precipitate your partner into a fall.

Your voice is a very effective weapon – practise shouting.

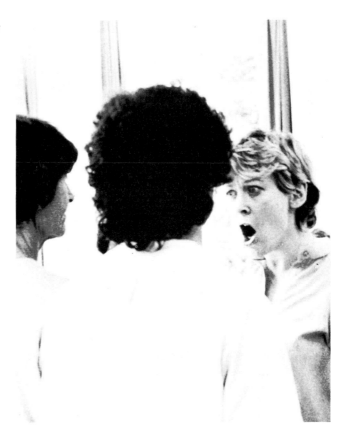

3
TACTICS FOR EVASION

If you achieve the feeling of fluidity in your body no one can hold on to you for very long.'

In judo, one of the first things to learn is to move our bodies as a unit: this is basic to all the techniques. You might think it was natural to move in this way, but often we are not aware of where all the parts of our bodies are, even though we intend them all to move in unison. This physical fragmentation can fragment our energy and keep us from being totally aware in any situation with which we have to deal.

Most of the exercises in Chapters 3–9 need a partner to practise with; ideally two partners – especially in the more complicated techniques – one playing the attacker, the second reading the instructions out loud. Try, too, to practise with different attacking partners so that you don't fall into a rigid pattern of responses.

Body Escape

When we have to evade danger, it is important not to make ourselves excessively vulnerable by having parts of our bodies dangling everywhere like hooks.

This exercise, which comes from judo, is comprised of the following three parts, each of which may be isolated in sequence in the following manner. Their purpose is to enhance both your intuitive and physical abilities to move out of the way of danger, to avoid being held by an attacker. You will need a partner for Part 1 and Part 3, but not for Part 2, which you can practise on your own before running through all three parts of this exercise in their proper sequence.

Part 1 – Maintaining Balance

1 Stand with your feet shoulder-width apart, shoulders back, chest relaxed, in the basic body escape position.

2 When you are ready, let your partner know.

3 In the following sequence you may move your base by stepping forwards, backwards, or from side to side, rather than becoming unbalanced by the push. Don't let your body bend at the waist, but try moving it as one unit by sliding your feet – one following the other, keeping the same distance between them as you move.

4 Work through the following sequence nine times. Each time your partner will increase the application of their strength. You are to think of the earth and maintain your balance.
Taking one step forward each time:
a partner nudges you from behind
b partner nudges you from front
c partner nudges you from both sides
d partner nudges you from back of left shoulder
e partner nudges you from back of right shoulder
f partner nudges you from front of left shoulder
g partner nudges you from front of right shoulder
h partner takes a step between your feet and attempts to lift you from under your armpits from front
i partner takes a step between your feet and attempts to lift you from under your armpits from behind

5 Go through this series nine times. Your partner should progressively push harder as you increase your willpower and feel more rooted in the earth.

6 Observe your physical and emotional response.

You may move your base by stepping forwards, backwards, or from side to side, rather than let yourself become off-balanced by the pushes. Try moving your body as one solid unit, by sliding your feet – one following the other, maintaining the same relationship of the distance between them as you move.

1

Part 2 – Moving Correctly

1 Stand in the basic body escape position as in **1** of Maintaining Balance, that is with your feet shoulder-width apart, shoulders back and chest relaxed.

2 Keeping your body straight, transfer your weight to the front half of your feet by bending your knees slightly. Do not lean forward to achieve this. Keep your eyes straight ahead, but don't stare: keep your eye muscles relaxed so that you can see to either side as far back as possible, as well as in front – developing peripheral vision is vital.

3 With one foot following the other as though they were connected with a thick piece of elastic, maintain the relationship between your feet by sliding one foot after the other in the following directions. Let the movement start from a point a little below your navel and a little inwards – this is your movement centre.
a forwards
b backwards
c side to side

4 Still keeping the weight in the front half of your feet by bending your knees slightly, as in **2**, pivot in the following directions.
a ninety degrees to the right and left
b one hundred and eighty degrees to the right and left

5 Now step forty-five degrees to the right with the right foot and pivot quickly. Make sure you are moving from and with your centre, as in **3**.

3b

6 Repeat **3–5** three times.

Part 3 – Evading Contact

1 With your partner 2 m (6 ft) from you, have them attempt to push you as in Maintaining Balance, steps **1–4**. This time, use the ways of escaping that you practised in Moving Correctly and think of water to maintain your fluidity. You and your partner should resume the same distance from each other between each push: the distance will sharpen your intuition and improve your sense of timing, so increasing your anticipation of danger and ability to move out of the way before it happens. Make sure that you are moving your body as a unit.

2 Exchange roles three times.

Get used to your partner pushing you and to responding differently, as in Parts 1 and 3 of the body escape exercise.

3 As you practise this more, decrease the distance between you – first 1 m (3 ft), then 30 cm (1 ft); then increase it – first 4 m (12 ft), then 6 m (18 ft), having your partner run at you from the greater distances. The shorter distances will improve your reflexes, and the greater ones will increase your awareness and intuition.

4 When you play the attacker, observe how it feels to pursue someone you cannot contact when you go to push or grab them. What happens when you attempt to grab water?

Using the Elements

When it comes to evading someone who is trying to hold or hit you, there are many types of movement you can use. Experiment with the following exercises until you find which you are most in harmony with. Practise evasion in this way until it is effective, then try to develop the other ways so that your technique is balanced. It is almost impossible to be grabbed or held when you put your whole spirit behind these movements.

Fire Evasions

1 Put yourself in a confined space, such as a kitchen or bathroom. Feel your base.

2 Feel the qualities of fire (page 64) through your body and begin expressing them. Change rhythm several times.

3 Now, for thirty seconds, ask your partner to attempt to grab you. First, just move your body without any particular technique, sending fire through your eyes – become a dragon. Fire needs oxygen to keep burning, so be sure to keep breathing properly.

4 Again, ask your partner to attempt to grab you. This time add your physical fire techniques – send fire out through all parts of your body. If your partner succeeds in grabbing you, hiss and keep moving.

Air Evasions

1 Allow the qualities of air (page 65) to permeate your mind and body, starting by paying attention to your breathing. Let air fill you up like a large balloon. Ask your partner to lift you. Was it easy for them?

2 Repeat using the qualities of earth (page 63), then water (page 63). Did you notice any differences?

3 Now go back to feeling like air, moving round the room lightly.

4 For thirty seconds, have your partner attempt to grab you. Keep escaping with movements like air. Was that easy or difficult for you to maintain?

Water Evasions

1 Just as water cannot be held onto, once you achieve this feeling of fluidity in your body no one can hold onto you for very long. Close your eyes and allow your body to fill up with the feeling of water's qualities (page 63).

2 When you have achieved this feeling, ask your partner for one minute to try to grasp onto you in different ways. Be sure to keep your feet flat on the ground and slide your base (page 88). Keep moving as water.

4
HOLDS AND ESCAPES

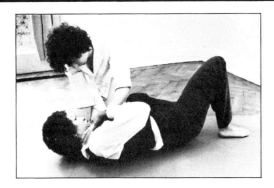

'Once you are aware of your will and how it works through your body, no one can hold you unless you allow them to.'

The more you practise escapes from holds, such as grips, chokes and pins, the more spontaneous your response will be, and the more the separate movements will develop into a relaxed, natural sequence.

Obviously, when you come to use the escape or any other techniques, you may have to do something else if you are still feeling threatened – a determined attacker who has not been immobilized is still a danger. For these *follow-throughs*, you can use any of your weapons (page 80) repeatedly, such as kicking (page 116), or more complex techniques, such as in choking from the front (page 100). Practise feinting (page 81) to learn what your attacker's response to different blows and kicks would be. This will help you anticipate the next target areas to be immediately exposed for more follow-throughs.

Follow-through is important for all the ways you stand your ground. Sometimes this means running away, or using your voice (page 84) to let the person know you will have no more of what they are doing. Remember that self-defence has to do with effectively *communicating* your worth and follow-through is essential to making this point.

Keep practising a repetition of techniques for follow-throughs, such as a series of kicks or a kick followed by thrusting the heel of the hand under the chin. For really dangerous situations I recommend using the following:
- double finger poke to the eyes (page 128)
- pressing the eyes into the back of the head (page 129)
- heel of the hand to the chin (page 126)
- knee or kick to the groin (page 121)
- grabbing and twisting the testicles (page 80)

Blending

Blending, rather than accentuating the conflict by pulling away, is an important element in dealing with an attack – think of water (page 63).

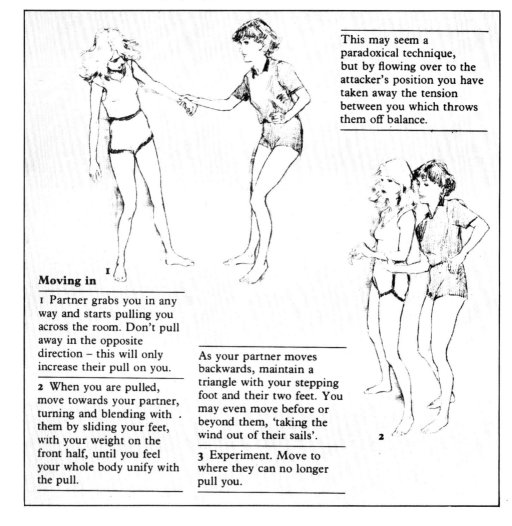

This may seem a paradoxical technique, but by flowing over to the attacker's position you have taken away the tension between you which throws them off balance.

Moving in

1 Partner grabs you in any way and starts pulling you across the room. Don't pull away in the opposite direction – this will only increase their pull on you.

2 When you are pulled, move towards your partner, turning and blending with them by sliding your feet, with your weight on the front half, until you feel your whole body unify with the pull.

As your partner moves backwards, maintain a triangle with your stepping foot and their two feet. You may even move before or beyond them, 'taking the wind out of their sails'.

3 Experiment. Move to where they can no longer pull you.

Grips

When someone has a grip on you, the balance of both you and your attacker is destabilised and you can use this to regain control of the situation.

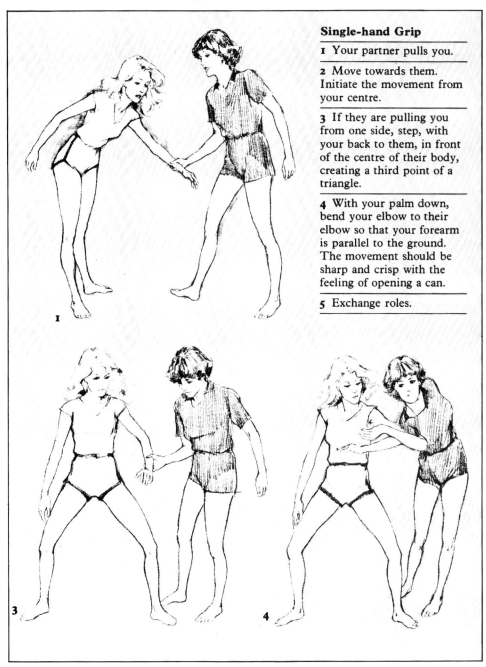

Single-hand Grip

1 Your partner pulls you.

2 Move towards them. Initiate the movement from your centre.

3 If they are pulling you from one side, step, with your back to them, in front of the centre of their body, creating a third point of a triangle.

4 With your palm down, bend your elbow to their elbow so that your forearm is parallel to the ground. The movement should be sharp and crisp with the feeling of opening a can.

5 Exchange roles.

Cross-wrist Grip 1

1 Your partner reaches across and grabs your wrist.

2 Extend the energy through your arm from your centre, as in the resilient arm exercise (page 17) and through the edge of your hand trace a wave, under to over your partner's wrist. As the edge of your arm and hand perform the wave, extend your palm as if it is a mirror, reflecting back to your partner their out of balance action. At the same time, take a cross step to behind them, with the foot on the same side of your body as you are being held. The distance you stay behind your partner will depend on the length of both your arms: this is the key for you to step to the place where you can keep your partner off-balance. Grab their wrist and continue the wave by turning their elbow up.

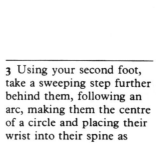

3 Using your second foot, take a sweeping step further behind them, following an arc, making them the centre of a circle and placing their wrist into their spine as high as it will go.

4 Follow-through by pushing them away.

5 Exchange roles.

If you are gripped with two hands, treat them as one and repeat **2** and **3**.

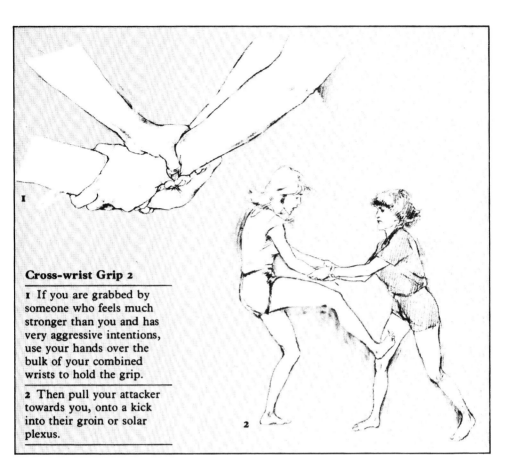

Cross-wrist Grip 2

1 If you are grabbed by someone who feels much stronger than you and has very aggressive intentions, use your hands over the bulk of your combined wrists to hold the grip.

2 Then pull your attacker towards you, onto a kick into their groin or solar plexus.

When your arm is gripped you can both free yourself and control your attacker.

Double-wrist Grip

1 Partner grabs you.

2 Keep your feet flat on the ground and bend your knees so that your centre is well below the strength of their grip.

3 From your centre, explode up like a volcano.

4 At the same time, bring your palms together like cymbals.

5 If you feel that the situation is still dangerous, you may follow-through with one or more of your weapons (page 91).

Chokes

These are very dangerous attacks – you can black out in five seconds, through lack of oxygen passing through your windpipe (trachea) and lack of blood and oxygen to the brain, passing through the carotid arteries (page 79). If you are being choked, or pinned and choked (page 106), do *not* put your head back – this will enable your attacker to exert real pressure on the vulnerable areas. The best way to protect these is to pull in your head and chin, making the muscles of your neck stand out. However, don't angle your head down when you do this – you won't be able to see properly in this position, it makes the back of your head a good target for your attacker to strike, and you will sacrifice your balance. If you can, use your chin sharp down into the soft V of your attacker's hand. As it is a very frightening feeling to be choked, you might want to prepare your neck for these exercises by touching and squeezing your own neck first.

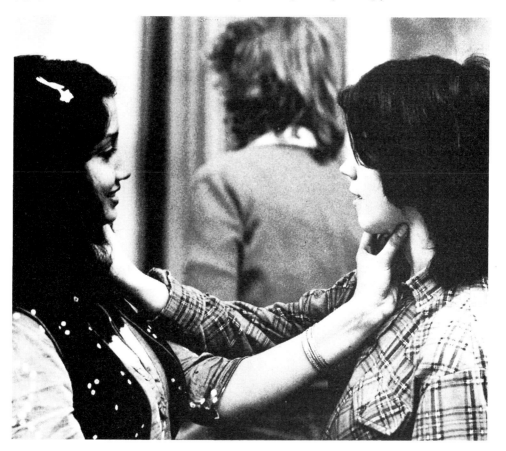

Get used to having your neck touched, so that you won't feel panic when practising techniques to escape being choked.

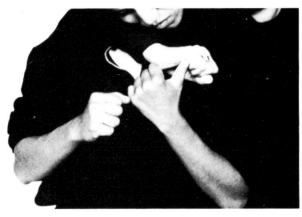

Once you have prised out your attacker's little finger, by hanging on to it you can keep them dancing around.

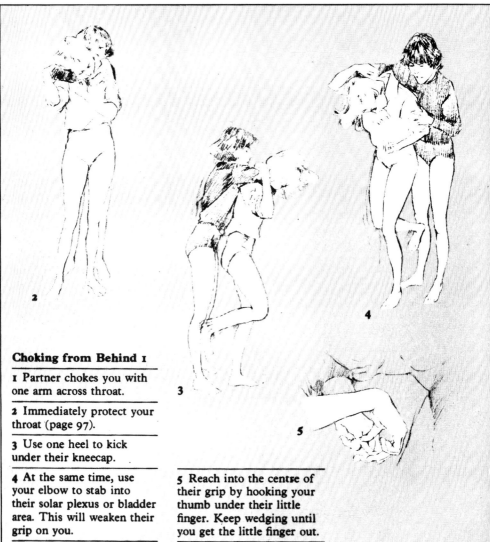

Choking from Behind 1

1 Partner chokes you with one arm across throat.

2 Immediately protect your throat (page 97).

3 Use one heel to kick under their kneecap.

4 At the same time, use your elbow to stab into their solar plexus or bladder area. This will weaken their grip on you.

5 Reach into the centre of their grip by hooking your thumb under their little finger. Keep wedging until you get the little finger out.

6 **6** Then swiftly swing their arm off by applying leverage to the joint.

7 If you can't get the little finger out, switch tactics. Use your other hand to grab the thumb part of their grip.

8 Shifting one shoulder up, and using your thumb as a guide, twist their arm and start to take it behind them.

9 Press it into their spine at their heart level.

10 If you want, after grasping a little finger and doing **6**, you can keep them moving around – 'little finger dancing' – by maintaining a downward pressure on the joint and pressing the finger towards their shoulder, forcing them away in any direction you choose.

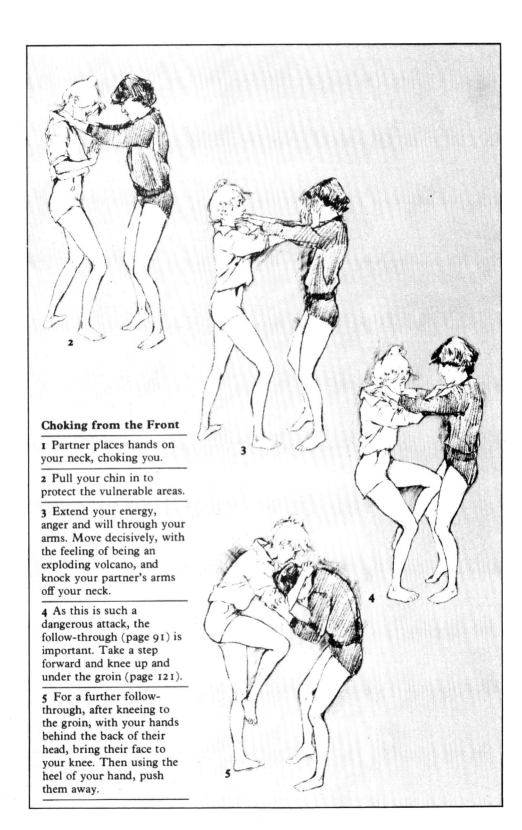

Choking from the Front

1 Partner places hands on your neck, choking you.

2 Pull your chin in to protect the vulnerable areas.

3 Extend your energy, anger and will through your arms. Move decisively, with the feeling of being an exploding volcano, and knock your partner's arms off your neck.

4 As this is such a dangerous attack, the follow-through (page 91) is important. Take a step forward and knee up and under the groin (page 121).

5 For a further follow-through, after kneeing to the groin, with your hands behind the back of their head, bring their face to your knee. Then using the heel of your hand, push them away.

You may be down to start with, but you can turn your attacker over.

Pins

Pick the moment that you feel safe to move against your attacker. All these escapes require determination and quick decisive movement. Use and channel your anger for assistance. When you have tried the pins on the following pages, work out other ones that could be used on you and how you could get out of them.

Once you are aware of your will and how it works through your body, it should be difficult for anyone to hold you unless you allow them.

Pinned on Stomach

1 Imagine your partner has pushed you down, or you were lying in bed. In addition, they will grab the back of your head, attempting to smash your face into the ground.

2 Try to avoid being actually pinned by getting off your stomach as soon as possible. Either come to your feet or turn onto your side. You have more advantage in resisting this way.

3 However, if they get a real hold on you before you can do this, quickly bring your elbows to your knees, making yourself into a ball which will push your back and pelvis up.

4 Roll your attacker onto their back.

5 You may follow-through, controlling them by holding onto one of their arms from the side.

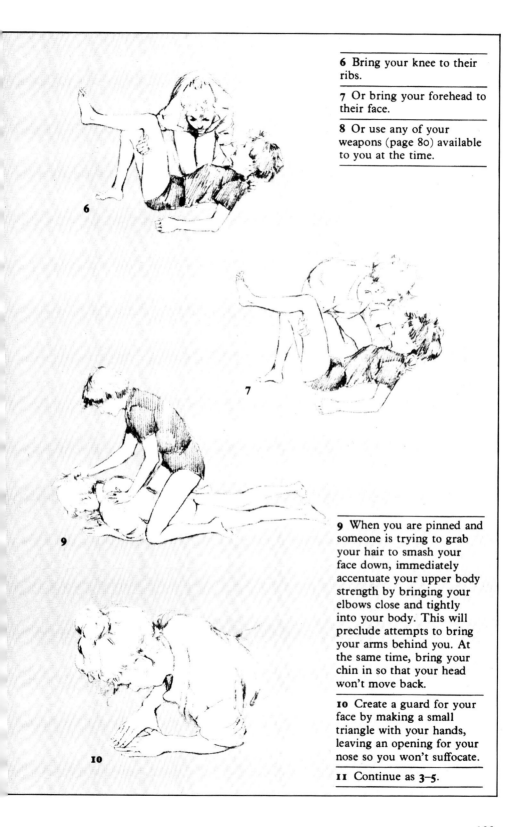

6 Bring your knee to their ribs.

7 Or bring your forehead to their face.

8 Or use any of your weapons (page 80) available to you at the time.

9 When you are pinned and someone is trying to grab your hair to smash your face down, immediately accentuate your upper body strength by bringing your elbows close and tightly into your body. This will preclude attempts to bring your arms behind you. At the same time, bring your chin in so that your head won't move back.

10 Create a guard for your face by making a small triangle with your hands, leaving an opening for your nose so you won't suffocate.

11 Continue as **3–5**.

Four-point Frustration Pin

Commonly done by brothers and male friends for play.

1 Lie on your back. Allow your partner to sit on you, pinning your wrists. Take a deep breath and remind yourself that you are still alive and have time to get out.

2 Bring your feet along the ground, close to your hips, lifting your hips. This will tip their balance forwards onto your wrists. At the same time, turn you head to the side. This is very important as otherwise you can injure your nose.

3 Your partner should be prepared to catch themselves as they are propelled forwards because this happens quickly.

4 Remove the target – your wrists – by fanning your arms straight down to your sides.

5 If you meet too much resistance, extend your arms up above your head and then fan them down.

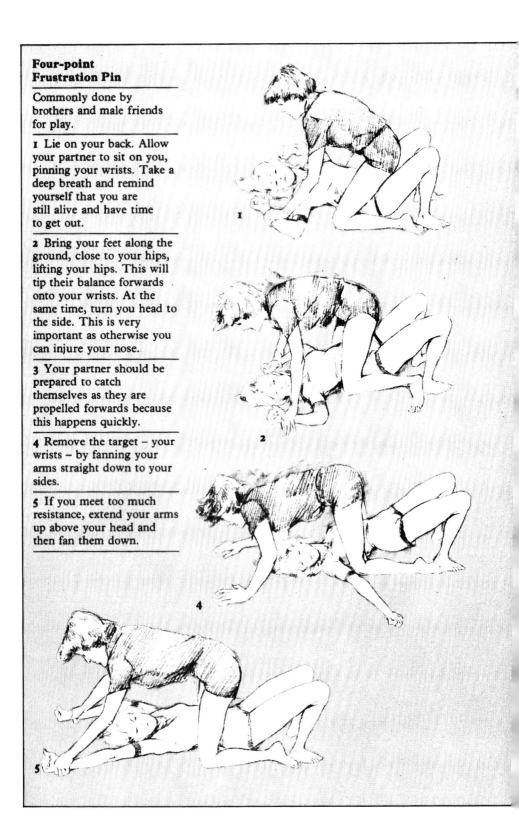

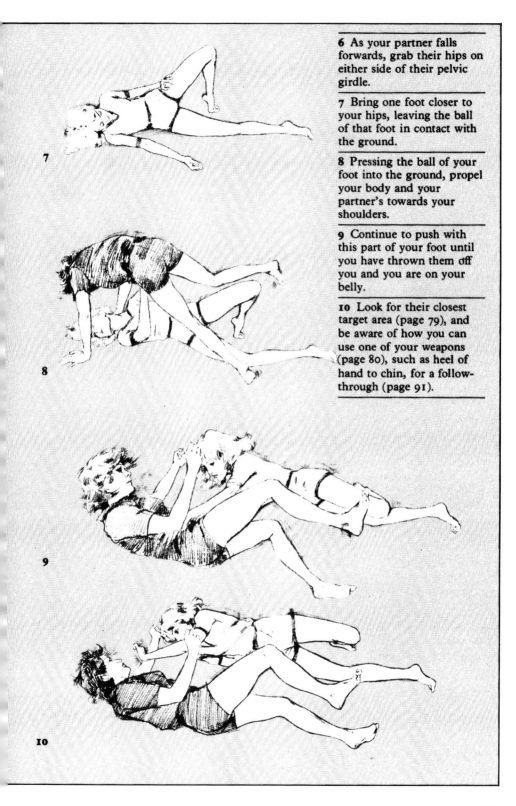

6 As your partner falls forwards, grab their hips on either side of their pelvic girdle.

7 Bring one foot closer to your hips, leaving the ball of that foot in contact with the ground.

8 Pressing the ball of your foot into the ground, propel your body and your partner's towards your shoulders.

9 Continue to push with this part of your foot until you have thrown them off you and you are on your belly.

10 Look for their closest target area (page 79), and be aware of how you can use one of your weapons (page 80), such as heel of hand to chin, for a follow-through (page 91).

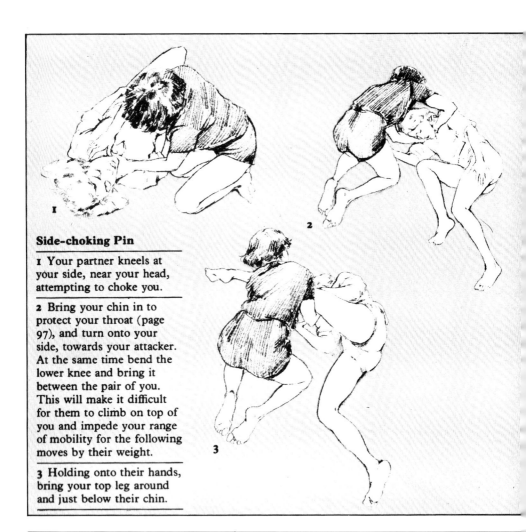

Side-choking Pin

1 Your partner kneels at your side, near your head, attempting to choke you.

2 Bring your chin in to protect your throat (page 97), and turn onto your side, towards your attacker. At the same time bend the lower knee and bring it between the pair of you. This will make it difficult for them to climb on top of you and impede your range of mobility for the following moves by their weight.

3 Holding onto their hands, bring your top leg around and just below their chin.

Underarm Pin

1 Stand with your feet shoulder-width apart.

2 Your partner comes up behind you, reaches under your arms and immobilizes your shoulders by clasping their fingers together behind your neck, then pushes your head down.

This pin is only made physically possible for an attacker to execute effectively if the victim reacts to this by screaming and throwing her arms up into the air.

3 Allow yourself to be a victim by reacting in the manner described above.

4 Repeat **2**, then resist by keeping your arms down and going tense and rigid – now your partner can pick you up like a useless doll.

5 Repeat **2** but bend your knees slightly and make yourself heavy; keep your shoulders down and elbows into your sides, maintaining the feeling that your chest muscles are pulling into your centre chest bone.

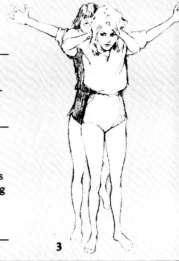

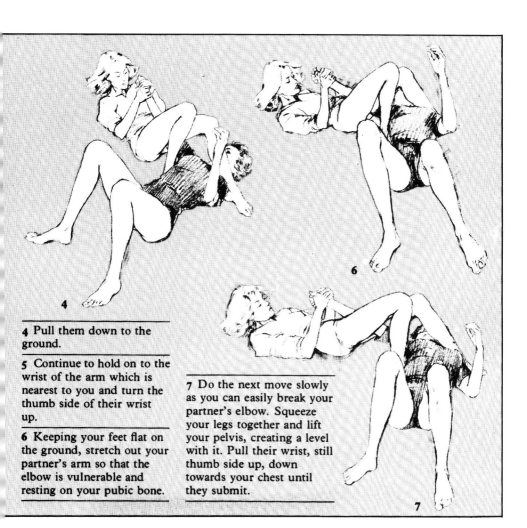

4 Pull them down to the ground.

5 Continue to hold on to the wrist of the arm which is nearest to you and turn the thumb side of their wrist up.

6 Keeping your feet flat on the ground, stretch out your partner's arm so that the elbow is vulnerable and resting on your pubic bone.

7 Do the next move slowly as you can easily break your partner's elbow. Squeeze your legs together and lift your pelvis, creating a level with it. Pull their wrist, still thumb side up, down towards your chest until they submit.

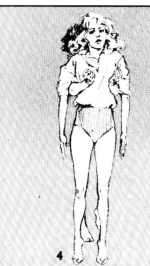

Extend your will down through your body into the earth: say no with your body. It should be difficult for your partner even to slide their arms under yours. If they have exceptionally long arms they may be able to touch their fingers behind your neck but there will be no power in the hold. They will not be able to immobilize you.

6 Now exchange roles and repeat **1–5**.

Group Attacks

Remember, in this situation your attackers are crediting you with power – they think it takes more than one to subdue you. When approached by more than one attacker, it may be possible to avoid being grabbed at all by using the swift, continuous, darting movements associated with fire (page 64).

Evading Groups

In most groups there is usually a leader and a few supporters. Try to get them in each other's way. Treat them as one energy source rather than fragmenting your energy by trying to respond to them separately, unless you want to concentrate on the individuals enough to identify them later.

If they do get hold of you, move with them to the point when they have a common goal, such as taking you to a car. The moment they start to blend is when you start moving like a tornado. Remember, you have your weapons (page 80), such as side kicks or bringing your heel back to their knees if they are holding your arms. As a general rule you should try to break free first, then use your weapons. But, again, do whatever works best *for you* at the time.

Treat a group as one energy source rather than as individuals.

5
LEARNING HOW TO FALL

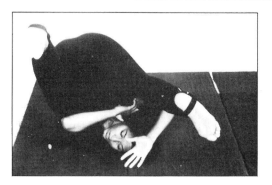

'Cultivate the attitude that you are blending into the earth rather than being knocked from an upright position.'

The exercises that follow are taken from aikido and judo – both these martial arts are built round one's ability to fall. The more comfortable you feel with falling, the more skilled you will become at throwing (page 130) because they are directly interlinked. One physical preparation that you can do is working on press-ups (page 45). Having a strong upper body can help prevent you being hurt in a fall.

Keypoints

- Feel the fluidity of water (page 63) within your body rather than seeing it as hard, having the potential to crash into or conflict with the earth below.

- Settle into the falls as though there was a cushion of air under you.

- Aim at making contact with the ground with the fleshy and muscular parts of the body rather than the bony ones.

- Upon contact with the ground, let the impact disperse in circles (see them in your mind, then feel them spreading out round your body).

Learn to view falling positively, not negatively – cultivate the attitude that you are blending down into the earth rather than being knocked from a rigid upright position. Also, when you fall, get back up immediately, as this will increase your emotional resilience or ability to 'spring back' during a crisis.

Getting up again immediately has two additional values from a physical point of view. By continuing your downward motion into an over and up one, you will lessen your impact on contact with the ground. Also, a curling-up, all-in-one movement leaves as little of you as possible exposed to the attacker, and removes you from his reach quicker. If pushed forward, try not to end up flat on your face, but gather yourself in and keep rolling. On your back, draw you legs up and keep rolling, backwards or sideways, or use your legs to kick out, rocking your body forward and up at the same time. Be prepared to come up at any angle, not just straight forward or straight back.

The psychological value of being able to accept being down as a momentary part of life's cycle is very great: it takes away from the shock, so negating your attacker's advantage.

In this competitive society, we are usually taught that being upright and on top at all times is important, and that being down is shameful and must be resisted. This leads people to become rigid and stagnant, afraid to move around and take risks for fear of falling. The fear manifests itself in physical resistance and brittleness, which means you will absorb more of the force of a blow instead of flowing away from it, or fall clumsily if pushed. And it manifests itself in people's attitude to life, having an ageing effect. Those who stay flexible and willing to take risks, to adopt unfamiliar mental positions temporarily in the interests of then being able to move on, change and progress, remain youthful and *survive crises*.

Another problem with learning to fall is having resistance to and fear of physically hurting oneself, imagining this to be the inevitable result of contact with hard, unnatural surfaces such as concrete. You can overcome this initially by using a carpet, mat or soft lawn while practising the techniques. But then you should move onto hard surfaces. Remember that these martial art falls were worked out in order to save people from being damaged and disadvantaged when they were thrown to the ground by an attacker. If you trust yourself when you do them, you won't be hurt.

The Wilting Flower

This fall is from aikido and its direction is backwards.

1 Stand with your feet shoulder-width apart in the body escape form (page 87). Feel the support of the earth under you as a soft cushion.

2 Extend your arms out from your body. Let them fill with energy, as in the resilient arm exercise (page 17). Keep your palms soft and parallel to the ground.

3 Support your full weight on one of your legs. Now turn the lower half of your other leg under you by pointing your foot and fold the extended leg under you. Using your arms for balance, settle down to the ground with the feeling of a descending lift. Be sure to bring your chin down towards your chest when you are half-way down. This will keep your head safe and will start to give your spine the necessary roundness for its protection as you roll backwards.

4 Curl into a ball and rock back, absorbing the momentum of the fall. Maintain the integrity of this form and allow your entire body the feeling of surrendering to the earth.

5 Use the backward momentum of the roll, your arms reaching as for a rope, to spring up to your feet and regain your balance.

You can control the speed of this fall to a great extent.

6 Now repeat this standing on the other leg. Practising with alternate sides increases your speed.

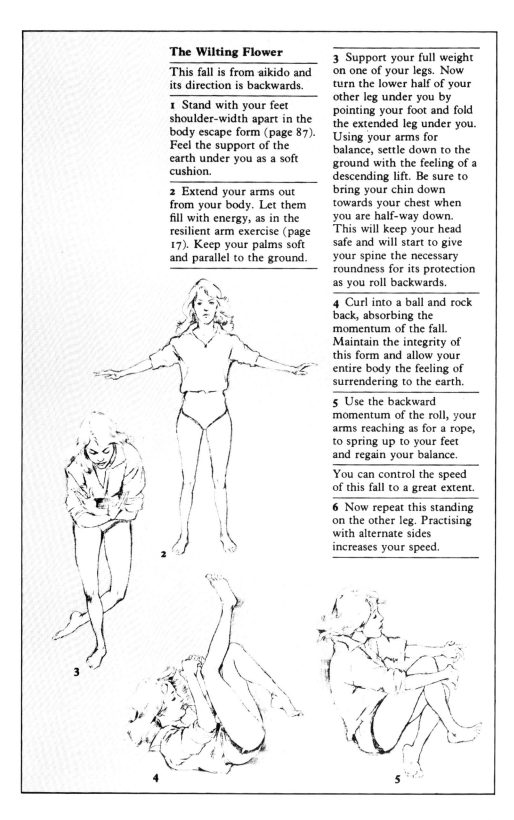

Side Sweep

This fall is also from aikido and its direction is to the side and back.

1 Stand in the basic body escape form (page 87).

2 Support your weight on one leg and, sweeping the other leg forty-five degrees with the hand on that side, settle down as you did in the wilting flower fall (page 111), pulling in your chin.

3. Rock back.

4 Stand up and regain your balance.

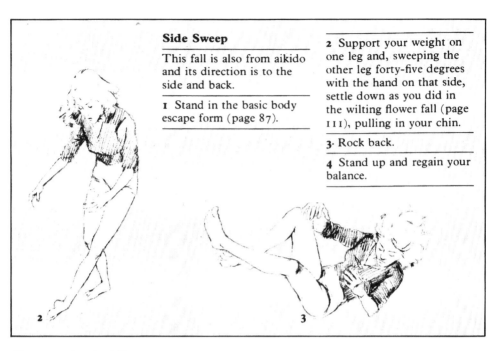

Keep repeating the falls until you can blend happily with the ground.

Triangular Forward Break

This exercise, which is based on a judo fall, should prevent injury to your knees, hips, collar bones, face and head. Working on press-ups (page 45) is a particularly useful preparation.

1 Do between five and twenty press-ups, along with some shoulder and neck stretching, to get your body and mind in the appropriate disposition.

2 Adopt a kneeling-sitting position.

3 Bring your chin to your chest. Keep your spine straight and shoulders loose.

4 From your knees, reach out and gently catch yourself, forming a triangle with your hands and forearms to support yourself.

5 Repeat 4. This time, though, lift your hips and lengthen your legs so that all that is touching the ground is your forearm triangular base, the balls of your feet, and the underside of your toes. Hold the position for about fifteen seconds so that you will develop strength within it.

6 Repeat this three times.

7 After you feel comfortable doing 3–5, do the fall from a standing position. Be sure to tuck in your chin and flex the muscles in your back, arms and buttocks to give support to your spine. Keep your spine straight and hips up. This is important for the protection of your lower back: do not let it sag.

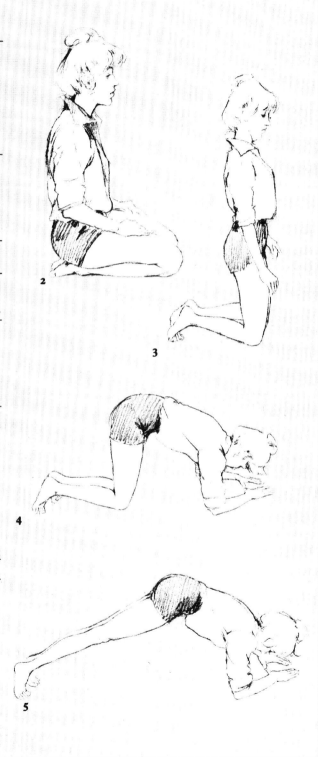

Use your foot to thrust your weight over into a roll.

Over the Shoulder Roll

This fall is from judo and aikido and can be done forwards or backwards. Its purpose is to prevent injury to the skeleton and organs of the body by absorbing the force of the forward or backward momentum.

1 Do some shoulder, neck and spine loosening.

2 Kneeling on the ground, turn your head to the left, placing your chin just below your left collar bone. Reach back past your left knee so that your shoulder tucks under.

3 With your chin, head and shoulder protected as in **2**, make yourself into a ball and carry yourself over. Roll on the diagonal of your back, not straight down the length of your spine, by carrying yourself over with the left leg and propelling yourself with the ball of your right foot.

4 Keep your right foot on the ground until you are three-quarters of the way over. This will give you a sense of grounding as you go over and will facilitate you in directing your fall.

Improving Technique

After you have become comfortable with all these falls, which is indicated by a soft and warm feeling in your chest and back, ask someone to work with you, pushing you in the appropriate directions. Maintain your balance as long as you can before falling. This will help you to assess how centred you are in dealing with external force.

Then go back to practising alone. Learn to generate more force and speed from within. Also expand your field of vision as you are falling. This will increase your ability to respond to force in a more balanced manner and will sharpen your intuition.

5 Repeat the roll, as in **3**. This time, watch the carrying leg until you complete the revolution. This will centre you within the roll, giving you a sense of balance even as you appear to be out of balance.

6 Now fold the carrying leg under as the propelling leg comes over it, with the foot flat in preparation for standing. This ground position in this roll should end with you on your side, not your back, and you get up from your side.

7 Repeat this sequence on the other side, reversing all the positions. Then alternate three times, gradually building up to nine times on each side.

8 This fall may be done from standing. However, as this form is more advanced, I recommend that it be done under the supervision of a qualified aikido instructor.

9 Go back to the wilting flower fall (page 111) and see how you may apply the same principles to falling backwards, rolling over your shoulder.

6
KICKING TO EFFECT

'Just by swinging the weight of your leg to an attacker's vulnerable areas you can have a lot of power.'

Legs and feet have some of the strongest muscles in the body. The swinging adult leg can deliver at least 45 kg (100 lb) of pressure while it only takes about 7 kg (15 lb) to severely injure, sprain, dislocate or fracture the kneecap. So, just by swinging the weight of your leg to an attacker's vulnerable target areas – especially the knee, shin and groin – you can have a lot of power. You can strengthen that power by practising. When you kick, the foot is an extension of the knee so, wherever the knee is aimed, that is where the power of your foot will be directed. You have to align yourself with your target area, both as to body angle and height up to which you bring your knee, as this is the level where your foot will strike. There are many kinds of kicks: I have chosen ones which require the least amount of training and balance to be effective.

Keypoints

- Keep a solid base.

- Kick from your centre rather than simply extending your leg.

- Maintain accuracy.
- Maintain balance.
- Upper body co-operation – keep upper body out of range of attacker's fists while still maintaining your balance.
- Protect your toes by pulling them back.
- Snap back quickly to a place of balance.
- Go swiftly and smoothly into a follow-through.

Always kick out from your centre, using your whole body.

Front Snap Kick

The best targets are under the kneecap and under the groin. Striking the lower ribs and face requires greater strength, balance and flexibility.

1 In preparation, do some leg stretches.

2 Stand with half your body exposed to the target on your partner, as explained in the Keypoints in Practising in the Body Weapons chapter (page 76).

3 Bend your knees. Acquire the feeling of sitting low into your legs, as though you are on a comfortable chair – drop all your weight into your legs.

4 Keeping low, direct yourself to the target with your centre and knee.

5 Lift your leg, bent, and pull your toes back. If you don't, because you are directing so much power through your foot, you could break your toes. Be aware of the ball of your foot as that will be the striking surface.

6 Shift your weight into your back leg so that you may use it for balance. Test this by simply lifting the kicking leg which should have no weight in it at this point.

7 Use your arms for balance and extend your foot. Do not throw it the first time: just get the feeling of how it will work. Hold that position for five seconds to check your balance.

8 To preclude having your foot caught, pull it back through your achilles tendon (back of heel) and stamp down. The front snap kick is not complete until your foot is snapped back.

9 Practise this ten times on each leg, using a wall instead of a partner, so that you can get the feel of connecting with a target. Aim at different targets, one after the other, bringing your foot back under your knee with a snap each time, before you put your foot down.

7

8

When you are really proficient, you can achieve more than one strike to each kick, if you are extremely swift and your balance is very good. Remember to re-direct your centre and knee towards each target.

10 You may further enhance your training and balance by practising with a moving target (page 83).

Backward Kick

Practise this against a solid wall that you don't mind getting dirty.

1 Maintain your balance on one leg while using your peripheral vision to locate the hypothetical target, such as under the kneecap. Do not turn your head all the way round as you need to see what is going on in front as well.

2 Swinging from your knee, kick back with your heel with the feeling of a donkey. Press your heel into the wall as hard as you can and hold it to a count of ten. This will add strength to your kick as this is a hard position in which to exert strength. Feel the muscles in your legs working, all the way up to your buttock.

3 Repeat this six times with each leg.

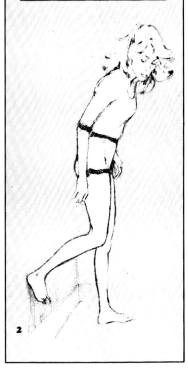

2

With a minimum turn of your head watch where you place your kicks.

Side Kick

This is particularly useful, not just if someone is standing at your side, but if one person is standing in front, with one or more at the sides. Kick the one in front with a snap kick, then kick to the side or sides, aiming at the knee, shin or instep.

1 Opening the pelvis, pivot your standing leg out about forty degrees, with the knee over it.

2 For balance, use your arms anyway you need to, including holding onto the attacker's arm. Using the outer edge of your foot to strike with, kick, say, the side of their knee, behind the edge of the kneecap.

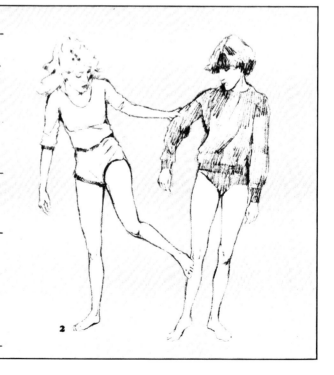

Kick or Knee the Groin

Don't be squeamish (page 81), you are being *attacked*. Be aware of your distance from the attacker's arms as he will instinctively go to protect his groin. You should either be close in to use the knee, as when he has his arms around you, or your leg's distance away from him so that you can throw a kick and snap back.

1 Your attacker's legs need to be open at least a couple of inches if you are to be assured of accuracy.

2 You can start by using the heel of your hand up and under his chin or nose.

3 This will bring him into a good position for delivering a kick or knee to the groin.

4 Once you have brought him into a good position, or if he is already in one, *you must not hesitate*. The strike must be delivered with one decisive move at the speed of a snap of your fingers.

5 Grabbing your attacker will bring him forward onto your knee or foot, increasing the force of the strike.

6 Kneeing can be done with your foot pointed.

7 Or it can be done with your toes up.

8 Immediately your attacker is disabled, don't hang around, run away as far as you can go.

If your legs are shorter than his arms, it would be more effective to use another body weapon in closer proximity, such as a kick under the kneecap, or a kick to the shin.

7
UPPER BODY STRIKES

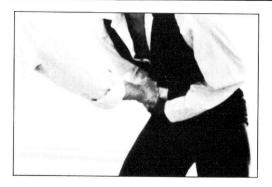

*'To maintain accuracy
think of striking through your attacker
rather than at him.'*

As you can see from the weapons and targets list (page 78), there are many upper body weapons. However, here I have chosen ones which require the least amount of training to be effective. Your partner should practise responding by feinting (page 81), so that you won't have to pull any of your punches. Seeing what the response to your blow would be also gives you reinforcing feedback. Repeat all the strikes several times, then do so from varying angles, then practise with the opposite side of your body. The elements most concerned with upper body strikes are earth, for grounding, and fire, for strength, speed, spontaneity and unpredictability.

Keypoints

- Keep a solid base.

- Move from your centre.

- Keep movement relaxed until the point of contact.

- Use mental power to aim through the target rather than stopping at it – this is the first step of a follow-through maintaining accuracy.

- Be accurate – look at the target, aim with your eyes first.

- Infuse and channel anger into the spirit of the appropriate symbol (page 80).

- Expose only half your body (page 77).

- Avoid communicating what you are going to do.

- Put the weight of your body behind the strike.

- Use your free hand as a guard and for balance.

Aim through your target and put the weight of your body behind the strike.

Making a Fist

To punch effectively and avoid injuring yourself, you must make a proper fist.

1 Extend your hand sideways.

2 Bend the fingers once, leaving your thumb up.

3 Bend them a second time, still leaving your thumb up.

4 Fold your thumb down and across to lock and squeeze the fingers, so supporting the striking knuckles – mainly the first two.

5 Clench your fist firmly but not so tight as to stretch the top skin of your hand.

6 Keep your wrist straight so that your fist doesn't bend backwards or forwards.

7 Do not clench your thumb inside your fingers or you may badly sprain or break it.

8 Do not clench your fist tightly in, tensing up the whole arm and shoulder.

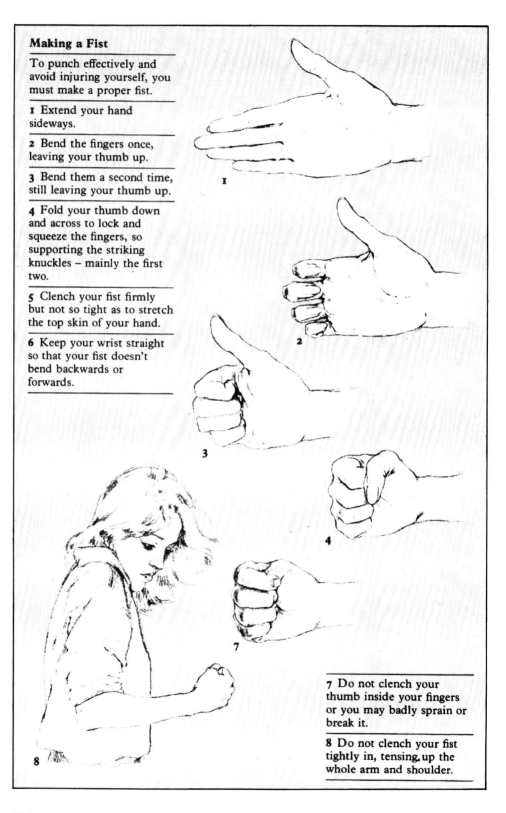

When making a fist to punch, don't clench it so firmly that the top skin of your hand is stretched, as here.

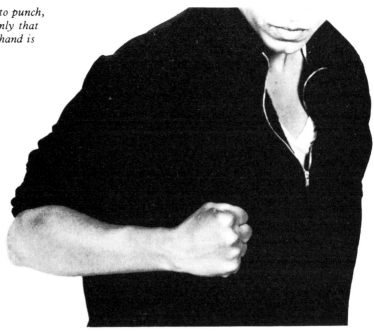

Punching

1 Establish your base by stepping forward with a sliding action, as far as the width of your shoulders plus half again. Bend the front leg only as far as the knee hangs over your toe. If you bend it further than that your punch will be off-centred and your balance will be too far forward. Swing your shoulders round as one piece behind the punch, keeping them sloping down and relaxed. Let your hand and arm be thrown from your shoulder as this will have more impact. Aim through the target, such as the solar plexus or face.

2 Repeat this ten times on each side. Each time increase your focus on punching with the weight emanating from the swinging action of your upper body.

1

Elbow Back

This can be used when someone is attacking you from behind.

1 Establish your base by taking a step back and dropping three-quarters of your weight into your back heel. The distance between your feet should be at least shoulder-width.

2 Using your peripheral vision, locate the target area, which can be the solar plexus or bladder.

3 Give support to the elbow you will strike with by placing your hand over your fist. Now push with the top hand as you strike with the elbow.

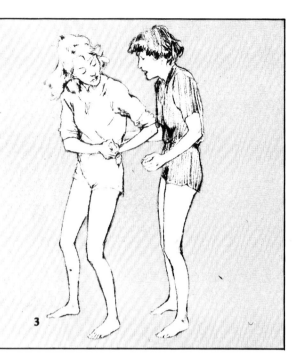

Heel of the Hand Thrust

This can be used when someone is squeezing you – or threatening to – from the front.

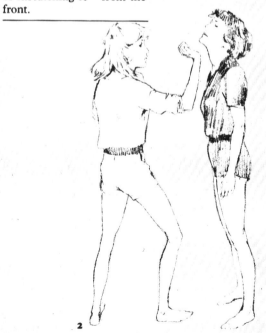

1 Flex your hand backwards so that it is almost perpendicular to your arm. This will expose the fleshy-covered heel of the hand.

2 Establish your base by stepping forwards and bending your knee. Then execute the thrust upwards under the chin or nose, with the feeling of a rocket.

3 If the size or position of the attacker requires you to use the full extension of your arm to make contact, it would be more efficient to use another weapon first. Pick one which is within immediate range of your strength, such as kicking the shin. Then, when the attacker responds to this by bringing his head down, follow-through with the heel of the hand.

Tiger Claw

Directed to the face, this can be used to ward off someone who is threatening you.

1 Assume the spirit of a tiger. The weight should most definitely be on the front half of your feet as tigers are very springy.

2 Bring your 'claws' out by stiffly curling your fingers. Tigers, other cats and bears all expose their claws before striking.

3 Establish your base by stepping out with the same leg. This time, turn your foot in slightly (about thirty degrees) to allow free range of movement. Keeping your elbow bent slightly, reach up, in front of you and slightly to the side. Now bring the full weight of your arm *diagonally* across and down to your opposite hip. Moving at a diagonal allows you a greater spectrum of territorial coverage.

4 You may enhance this strike by hissing like a cat.

Sweep your 'claws' down in an arc as you spring forward, hissing.

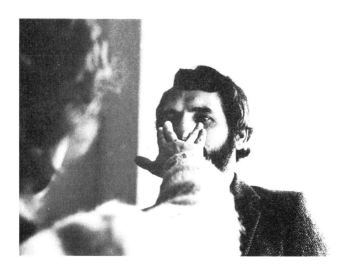

Simply lifting your hand gently into position, practise in front of your partner's face spacing your fingers correctly so that they would strike both eyes.

Double Finger Poke

Directed to the eyes, this can be used to ward off someone who is threatening you.

1 Assume the spirit of an attacking cobra.

2 Open your extended fingers into a V. Using all four fingers is better than using just two because the outer pair give strength and support to the inner pair. Also, you are fragmenting your energy by holding two fingers back. If you find it difficult to get either of your hands into this position, use the other hand to train the poking hand by opening the fingers in the middle.

3 Take a sliding step forward to establish your base. Then extend forward with your arm as though you were lunging with a sword. Once again, extend a little beyond the target, like a cobra striking and inserting its venom.

4 Finish by springing your hand back to your chest, and stepping back.

5 The eyes are one of the most vulnerable parts of the body, and people are very protective of them, so you may never have to make contact to get the aggressor to back away. However, to be successful, your intention must be one hundred per cent behind the movement.

Pushing Eyes into Skull

You could use this if your life is being threatened – perhaps someone is choking you and both his hands are occupied, or trying to rape you and his head is close to yours.

1 If you can reach, clasp your fingers behind the attacker's head. Otherwise, just hold the sides of his head and use your thumbs to press his eyes in, towards the back of the skull.

2 Don't worry – you will not end up with an eyeball dangling on each thumb. This action will cause the fluid in the eye to exert pressure on the retina which will cause shock to the brain and a temporary blackout. Press very gently on your own eyes to feel the potential of this weapon.

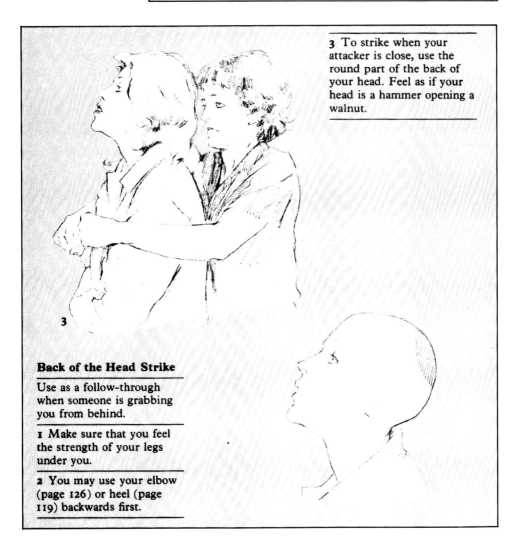

3 To strike when your attacker is close, use the round part of the back of your head. Feel as if your head is a hammer opening a walnut.

Back of the Head Strike

Use as a follow-through when someone is grabbing you from behind.

1 Make sure that you feel the strength of your legs under you.

2 You may use your elbow (page 126) or heel (page 119) backwards first.

8
THROWS

'The aggressor is already off-balance – so if you get him at the right point he will inevitably fall.'

Using your knowledge of the elements (page 60), you may think of an attacker as being light. When someone attacks you, he is out of touch with his own personal security, his own ground. Turn this to your advantage: once you position yourself below his centre of balance – usually his hip – and fit in tight, blending with him, you may direct his force, even if he is larger than you, wherever you like, as you will see in the following throws, which are taken from judo.

Prepare yourself to propel someone's whole weight by throwing a football. See how you bend from the knees (a must in all throws), and use your weight to launch the ball away from you. The keypoint in throwing someone is to decide where on your partner's or attacker's body, in any given position, the fulcrum is. That is the point against which you apply leverage, by thrusting, swinging or pulling, in order to tip them enough off-balance for them inevitably to fall by virtue of their own momentum.

Practise with someone who knows how to fall, and work on mattresses or mats – this will prevent your partner being hurt and enable you to be more realistic in sending them flying.

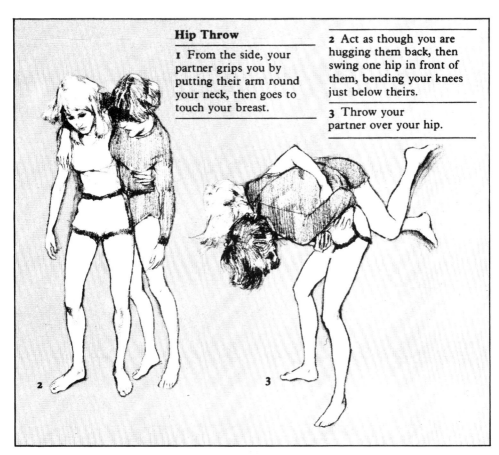

Hip Throw

1 From the side, your partner grips you by putting their arm round your neck, then goes to touch your breast.

2 Act as though you are hugging them back, then swing one hip in front of them, bending your knees just below theirs.

3 Throw your partner over your hip.

By picking the correct point to apply a thrust, you can use an attacker's weight to make them fall.

Once you have your attacker on the ground you can make your escape.

Inner Leg Hook

1 Partner squeezes you from the front, pinning your arms.

2 Step on their instep with your heel.

3 As a reaction to the pain they will grab the leg that you stepped on behind the knee.

4 Hook one leg behind the knee of their standing leg and pull it from under them.

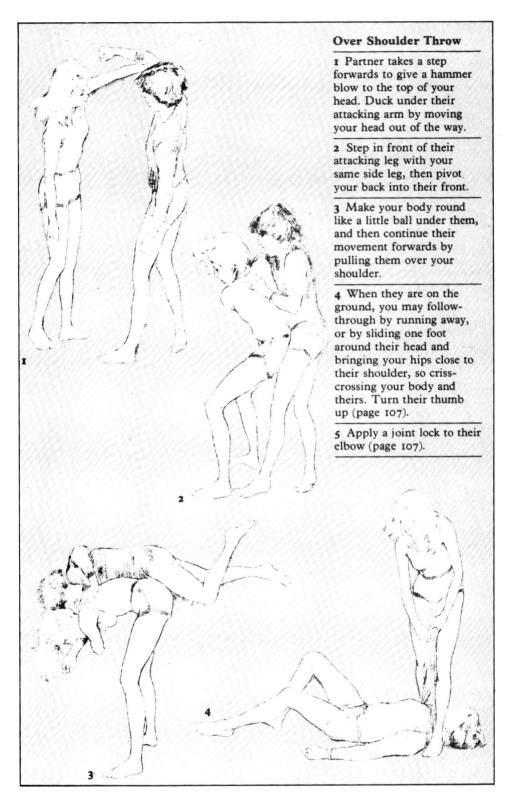

Over Shoulder Throw

1 Partner takes a step forwards to give a hammer blow to the top of your head. Duck under their attacking arm by moving your head out of the way.

2 Step in front of their attacking leg with your same side leg, then pivot your back into their front.

3 Make your body round like a little ball under them, and then continue their movement forwards by pulling them over your shoulder.

4 When they are on the ground, you may follow-through by running away, or by sliding one foot around their head and bringing your hips close to their shoulder, so criss-crossing your body and theirs. Turn their thumb up (page 107).

5 Apply a joint lock to their elbow (page 107).

Groin Throw

1 Partner is attacking you from the front. Don't resist, grab their arms.

2 Protect your head and neck by pulling them in as in chokes (page 97) and, holding on to their arms, settle down onto the ground with your bottom close to your heels. Keep the resilient arm feeling (page 17) in your arms.

3 Lift one leg and push your attacker over your head onto the ground.

4 To deal with someone who is choking you, follow through with a kick up into the groin.

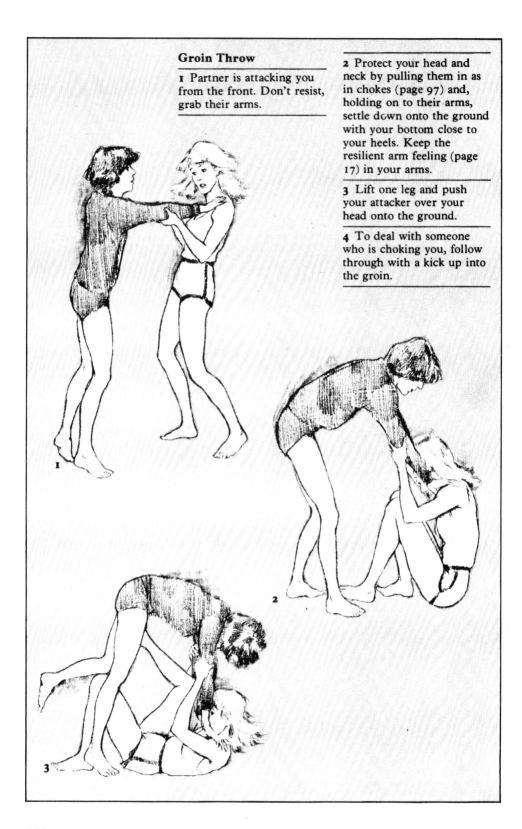

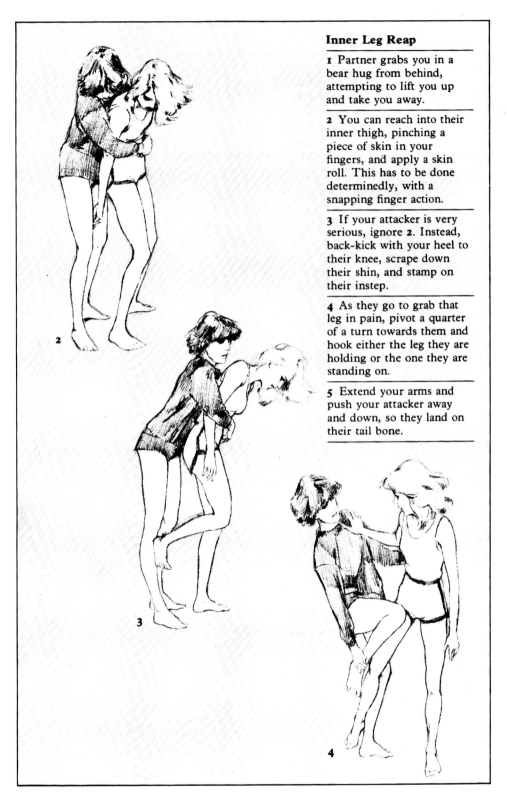

Inner Leg Reap

1 Partner grabs you in a bear hug from behind, attempting to lift you up and take you away.

2 You can reach into their inner thigh, pinching a piece of skin in your fingers, and apply a skin roll. This has to be done determinedly, with a snapping finger action.

3 If your attacker is very serious, ignore **2**. Instead, back-kick with your heel to their knee, scrape down their shin, and stamp on their instep.

4 As they go to grab that leg in pain, pivot a quarter of a turn towards them and hook either the leg they are holding or the one they are standing on.

5 Extend your arms and push your attacker away and down, so they land on their tail bone.

9
DEALING WITH KNIVES

'A weapon is an extension of the body – it has no power alone.'

If you are being attacked by someone armed with a knife, don't imagine that just by being 'nice' to the attacker and going along with his wishes you will escape without physical damage. It is highly likely that after he has done what he wants he will further terrorise you and then mutilate you for fun, or attempt to kill you – either because he has transferred his revulsion at his own actions on to you, or in order to stop you identifying him later. In all probability, you won't have anything to lose by fighting back, at the right stage.

Dealing with an armed attack

So, what do you do when someone is threatening you with a knife? First of all, realize that when someone has to use a lethal weapon on you, they are feeling pretty insecure inside and overcompensating for this with an air of over-confidence. But this 'confidence' is brittle, as they have to hide behind a weapon instead of dealing with you barehanded. This gives you a certain psychological advantage, provided that you can stay cool enough. Think of other reasons why someone would use a weapon on you. Perhaps they are after your possessions rather than your life, or maybe they are after your body to humiliate you so that they can feel more dominant. Are they experts with a knife, or will they be clumsy if they actually try to use it instead of just brandishing it around? As it is easy to freeze up when you become aware that someone may have a weapon, asking these questions to demystify the fear is the first step to coping with a knife attack.

The next step is to confront and demystify the weapon at your leisure. Familiarize yourself with your houseknives. How do they work? What kind of pressure is required to slash or stab different surfaces with different types of knives? – sometimes a surprisingly little amount. How could you deflect or intercept that pressure? Incidentally, *never* leave knives or scissors out to hand in your home where an intruder could grab them to use as a weapon.

Keypoints

- Respect the potential power of the weapon.

- Be aware of where the knife is at all times.

- Control the person holding the knife psychologically or physically.

- Try to assess what it is the attacker wants. Co-operate with their wishes in order to distract them as this is where they become off-balance. Basically if you can distract the attacker's mind, you have control of the weapon. This distraction can be mental or physical.

- An attacker with a knife is either very focused on that weapon, or on getting what they want. You may be able to take advantage of this narrow concentration.

- Go along with your attacker's wishes *until you feel safe enough* to move against him.

- A weapon has no power alone. Therefore, begin to see the weapon as an extension of the person's wrist and arm. If you can physically control the arm, especially the wrist, you have control of the weapon.

- In any knife attack, be prepared to use anything to hand to help you.

- Knock the knife out of their hand with any bag or books you are carrying.

- Use cushions, towels, bedding to cover and deflect the knife point, and/or to cover the attacker's head.

- Use any heavy clothing lying around or, if you are asked to strip, use the first substantial enough item you remove – such as a jacket – to cover and deflect the knife point, and/or cover the attacker's head.

When you are practising the exercises, think of the earth to make you strong enough to gain control, and water to keep you fluid enough to escape. Practise with a rubber toy knife – this enables your partner to slash and stab at you realistically instead of holding back, and you to establish the correct distance and timing for your moves.

There are no instant answers to dealing with knives. Though, for your purpose now, I suggest developing a strong foundation of demystifying the attacker with a weapon, along with an understanding that the weapon is an extension of his body – it has no power in and of itself.

Addendum to Fig. 4
Pounce like a tiger onto their wrist with your left hand and push the attackers arm down. Immediately, strike to their face under their nose to distract their attention and to off-balance them as you prepare to disarm the attacker.

Brandishing Knife

1 Partner brandishes knife.

2 Extend your arms to give you balance.

3 Move with your partner until you feel the opening to step in, forty-five degrees to their arm, so you have gone *behind* the point of the knife.

4 Grab their wrist and extend the thumb part of your grip into the V between their thumb and index fingers. Press firmly in there and quickly twist their arm into a joint lock.

When a knife is being used against you, to gain control of it, get control of the attacker's wrist.

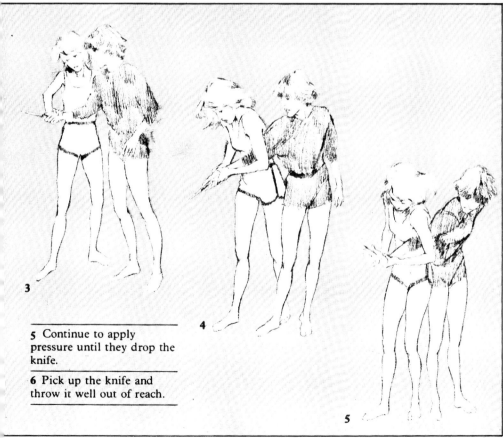

5 Continue to apply pressure until they drop the knife.

6 Pick up the knife and throw it well out of reach.

Knife at Your Back

1 Partner aims knife at your back.

2 Pivot quickly, escaping the path of the knife.

3 Make absolutely sure where the knife is.

4 Sieze the wrist of the attacking arm.

5 Apply a joint lock, such as on the elbow.

6 Or use a throw, such as the outer leg reap (done with a scything motion – like the inner leg reap, page 135).

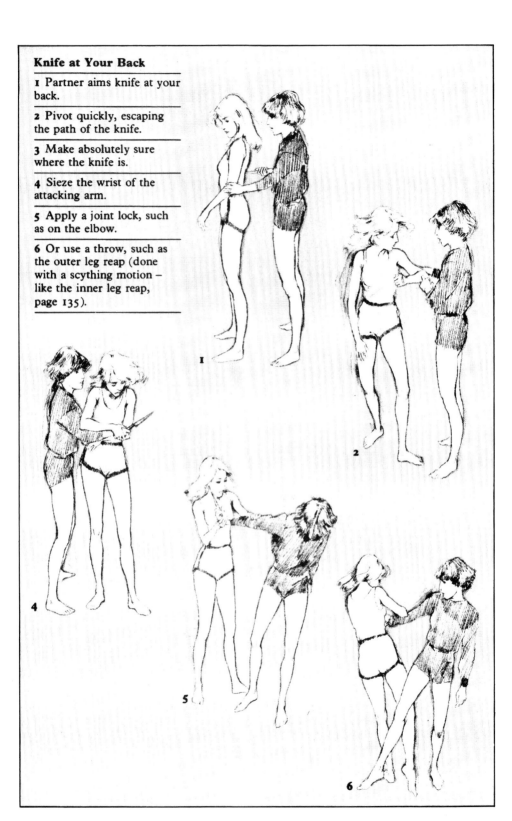

Knife at Your Throat from Behind

1 Partner moves in behind you and threatens you with knife, arm around your throat. Be aware of the blade of the knife.

2 Move your neck more into the crook of the attacker's elbow so that your neck is out of danger.

3 It is *extremely important* to take hold of their wrist so they won't cut your throat or face as you kick to their shin or kneecap and/or deliver an elbow to their solar plexus to weaken their hold on you.

4 Maintain your grip into the V of theirs.

5 Direct the attacker's hand with the knife into their back at heart level.

6 Use the outer edge (side blade) of your foot to kick behind their knee so that they fall forwards. Continue pressing your thumb into the V of their grip and take the knife with the other hand, throwing it well out of reach.

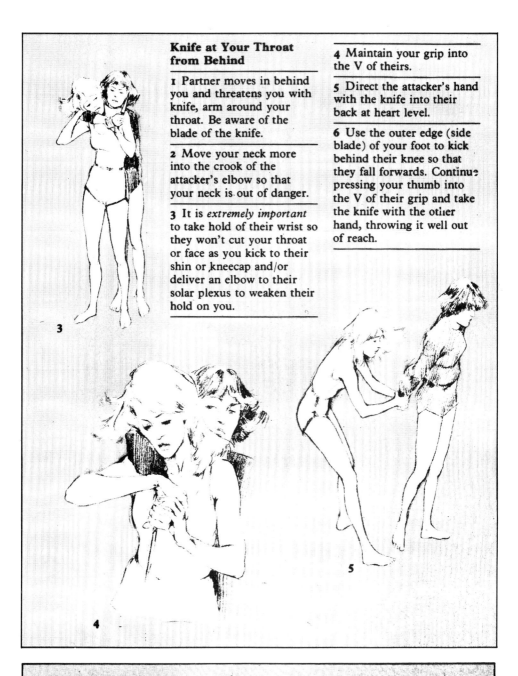

Lying Down Attack

1 Partner is straddling you, probably on your bed, threatening you with a knife at your throat.

2 Appear to listen to their demands, then pick the earliest *safe* moment to move, such as when they begin to unzip their trousers or are focusing on your crotch.

Use what you have learned so far in the pins on the ground (page 101) and knife deflections.

PHASE 3
MOVING ON

'To be free in our most basic territory is to have reached the dawn of our freedom as individuals.'

1
WHERE DO YOU GO FROM HERE?

Sweep violence off the streets!

> 'Self-preservation is an ongoing process of awareness; it spreads into all aspects of your life.'

What do I mean by 'moving on'? In Phase 1 I set out for consideration basic attitudes to self-preservation, and in Phase 2 I suggested techniques for physical self-defence. But the subject does not come to a tidy end there. Self-preservation is a continuing process of awareness. Once this process has started, it spreads into all aspects of your life, leads you to re-evaluate everything, increases your understanding of what is happening to you, your control over your life, and your will-power. So, I am talking about moving on:

- from living in fear to refusing to see yourself as a victim
- from denying the validity of your feelings to trusting your intuition
- from isolation in suffering to awareness of how widespread oppression is through violence and fear of violence
- from considering rape in the narrow sense of a sexual assault to taking a broader view of it as all violation.
- from watching the stranger in the street to thinking about the attitudes of men you are involved with
- from reacting to figures of reported crime to reflecting on all aspects of male aggression

- from individually acquiring physical techniques to co-operating with other women in refusing to accept the social set-up which permits attacks
- from accepting whatever a self-defence teacher says to being discriminating about with whom you learn
- from feeling that it is somehow women's fault if they are attacked, beaten or raped to campaigning for changes in the laws to give better protection and compensation
- from acceptance of male violence to working to change attitudes – of the next generation if nothing else

What is Rape?

Rape and self-defence are terms that people define very narrowly, yet they both have far-reaching implications. Self-defence is typically approached from the defence aspect rather than that being taken in conjunction with greater understanding of *self*. When it is approached primarily from the defence or technical aspect many of the important keys are omitted. These are attitudes, intuition, self-esteem, relationships, community responsibility, our connection with nature, and basic social conduct. As this extended perspective involves a blending of these elements, including the psychological and physical, I often refer to it as self-preservation.

Parallel with this expanded definition of self-defence must go an expanded view of the idea of rape. *All* violation is a form of rape. By increasing our awareness of this implication we consequently increase our patience and understanding of other people's struggles on all fronts, as well as our own.

This broader view begins with self-examination. Women, examine ways that you have and are being violated and work together with others to overcome these aggressive forces plus your vulnerability to them. Help a woman who has been physically raped by giving her support and asking her what *she* wants to do. This will begin to give her back her sense of self-worth. Encourage her with the fact that she survived. Encourage her to change her fear into anger.

Men, learn to find strength through expressing emotions – particularly the softer ones, such as fear, sadness, vulnerability and tenderness. Encourage other men to do the same. When you hear men talking about women in an abusive, derogatory or dismissive way, begin to take responsibility for making them aware of what they are doing.

Parents, be careful not to deprive your children of their own self-reliance by filling them with your fears and limitations. This is usually done through laying down rules and blanket do's and don'ts. Instil within them a foundation of resourcefulness by asking them questions such as, 'What do you think . . . how do you feel about that?' This will increase their emotional and psychological agility. It will also breed tolerance and appreciation for those who are different.

Those of us who suffer racial discrimination must increase our awareness of self-worth, of the beauty of our cultural heritage. Based on this, we should be demanding to live rather than just survive.

Senior people, begin to value your age as a tremendous treasure chest of willpower and strength, rather than as something which makes you useless. Take pride in the wisdom you have gained.

Although rape has manifested itself most extremely by male sexual assault on women, we all have the potential to do it in some form. The actual physical expression of it is simply a culmination or blown-up version of simpler attitudes and actions, based on lack of respect for others.

How many times have you picked up a child, taken their grounding away, without first asking their permission? Well, someone bigger than yourself could do the same with the same attitude.

How many times have you said yes when you really meant no? Said 'I can't' or 'You can't' or 'We can't', when you really meant 'I am afraid of being successful at this'? Said 'I should' rather than 'I will' or 'I won't'?

Knowing now that self-defence means taking responsibility for your own life, its safety and values, we should no longer expect daddy, the state, big brother or the police to manage our lives for us. Each of us holds the key to our own strength, safety, and community development. Self-defence is a social responsibility which begins with our relationship to self and then extends to our relationship with family and others.

There is constant pressure in our society to be a party to violence and violation – to accept it as 'the way things are' when we are the object, to acquiesce in its infliction on others, to inflict it. But we can refuse to be part of the system, either in the role of victim, or observer, or aggressor. When you hear the recurring messages – 'Times are hard and times are tough, and the only way you can make it is to be rough' – just listen to your intuition and you will stand your ground.

2
SELF-PRESERVATION A NECESSITY AND A RIGHT

'Self-defence begins with your taking an active part in defining your needs.'

The great surge in interest shown by women in learning to defend themselves is part of women's increasing self-assertiveness and refusal to accept either male violence or restraints on their freedom. Concern about self-preservation also results from sheer necessity – more women nowadays have to be out and about on their own and live alone. For example:

- Some 25% of all households in Great Britain now consist of a person living alone and the percentage is higher in inner city areas.
- In 1985 12% of families were headed by a lone mother.
- Between 60% and 70% of women under retirement age either work or are looking for work.
- Because of the general shortage of jobs and changing social circumstances there is an increase in the number of women – such as single mothers, older women unexpectedly returning to the labour market after divorce, wives of unemployed men – who cannot be choosy about the location and/or hours of the jobs that they can get.

And what about women's reactions to the idea that they accept restraints on their freedom of movement and the violence that they have to deal with in their lives? As with many other aspects of women's experience, once they start being brought out into the open through women discussing with each other what has happened to them and realizing the common basis of what they have been enduring, once women decide that it is just not good enough – there is no going back. You cannot wipe out awareness once it exists, or repress indignation and righteous anger once it has surfaced. And it is hard to negate growing feelings of self-worth.

These changes in attitude were highlighted for me by contact with one of the groups of Asian girls in Britain who are studying self-defence. These girls had a lot to overcome. There were the usual conflicting expectations about women's vulnerability and lack of importance but responsibility for being in the wrong place at the wrong time, plus strict family and religious expectations about the girls protecting their sexual purity and reputations while remaining modest and compliant in their demeanour, plus racial prejudice and the problem of being viewed as obvious targets – shy, nervous and weak. The older women in their community said, 'If we go out late, we have to take our men with us.' The younger girls confirmed that, 'For us, there is always fear in the streets.' Yet these girls were not prepared to live with all that. After organizing self-defence training they were saying: 'I feel more confident when I scream – it gives me aggression and will shock my attacker . . . I am still afraid of rape, but not as frightened as I was before self-defence classes . . . I can protect myself.'

The new demand by women for self-defence instruction has been related to the apparent growth of violent crime, child abuse, sexual assaults and rape. For instance, in England and Wales in 1986 crimes of violence against the person rose to 125,499 against 94,960 for 1979. Rape cases went up from 1,234 in 1978 to 2,288 in 1986. But a connection is unlikely as violence against females has always been under-reported. Various research in America and Britain has found that over one-third of women have been raped or sexually assaulted in some way, and that 50–70% have experienced male violence – figures which bear no relation to reports of these crimes, past or present. It is, therefore, highly questionable whether it is crime rates against women that have increased or simply willingness to report.

Whatever the position, a larger number of women have been prepared to seek justice for their violent treatment of all kinds. Perhaps these women thought changes in police guidelines and reforms in the law would guarantee them fairer treatment and make reporting less traumatic.

But, because reporting can still be an unnecessarily harrowing ordeal, there is a danger others may be put off in future. Problems that still continue are: certain police forces and some individual officers are unsympathetic and dismissive; legal procedures are lengthy, unpleasant and confusing; lawyers find ways of bringing up a woman's sexual history in court; verdicts and sentences are unpredictable; victims cannot feel safe from retaliation; and the media sensationalize cases, publish irrelevant details and do not protect the anonymity of rape victims.

Whether women choose to report violence or not, fewer are accepting their treatment meekly. First, there is a growing interest in self-assertiveness training and in countering all forms of sexual harassment that women are subject to, however apparently trivial. Then there is a huge increase in women studying self-defence – whether in special short courses or taking up one of the martial arts with great dedication. Incidentally, can we knock on the head the persistent myth that 'a little training is worse than none at all' – in other words, don't bother. Any increase in your awareness and belief that you can defend yourself are a help, and women police officers doing self-defence training reported that it was starting to be effective after only three to four hours of practice.

Women take up self-defence as a preventative measure or because they have been attacked and are not going to be helpless again. Many probably feel that being able to deal with an assailant directly is more effective than going through the distressing and possibly unproductive business of reporting what happened.

Another way of dealing with attackers that women may feel they want to try as well as reporting to the police, and better than individual effort, is to act through the community. The London Rape Crisis Centre publish a list of preventative steps in which the community can participate, and also suggest publicizing the fact that a man is a known rapist.

In California, the Santa Cruz Women Against Rape group gather together community members (especially women) to confront known rapists at their homes or places of work. The purpose of this is not to allow the man to escape the consequences of what he has done, but to let him know that the community will not tolerate this type of behaviour. Perhaps we should consider whether forms of action like this might have a more positive effect than that achieved by prison sentences?

Should we also be asking ourselves whether men are

inherently aggressive, or whether they learn violence as a result of the pressures in an aggressive and competitive society where nature itself is treated destructively? Certainly it seems that in those tribal societies where people are close to their natural environment there is less role distinction, women are respected, and there is little or no violence of any kind. Whereas, in those tribal societies where rape is rife, violence in general is a way of life. Equally, in crime- and-violence-prone, modern, inner-city sub-cultures, antagonism between the sexes, and rape as a way of deliberately expressing that, figure highly. In a well-known study of rape in Philadelphia, 71% of rapes were found to be planned and 90% of the rapists belonged to lower socio-economic groups, living in districts where there was a high degree of violent attacks generally.

This seems to refute the myth that rapists are crazy, anti-social strangers, who attack at random, prey to their sudden overwhelming desires. According to Rape Crisis Centres 65–75% of all rapists are known to the women they attack; rapists can be husbands, lovers, fathers, employers, the boy next door or the man who comes to read the meter; some 63% of rapes are planned; less than 2.5% of convicted rapists are mentally disturbed.

American statistics show that some half of wives have been physically abused by their husbands, 10% having been subjected to extreme violence. The women who come to Chiswick Family Rescue will, on average have suffered 35 batterings before they do so. Women's Aid say one quarter of all reported violent crime is that of men assaulting the women they live with. And of all female homicide victims, 40% are wives killed by their husbands. Given that rape within marriage is not illegal in most of the British Isles, and rarely prosecuted in Scotland, and that most battering does not result in criminal charges, the extent of violence within the home can be imagined.

If it is true that some of the ordinary, sane men we know are capable of acting like this if allowed to, then *we cannot afford the luxury of being weak*. Our mental attitudes about self-preservation and our feelings of self-worth, our ability to defend ourselves physically, together with respect for what our intuition tells us, are *critical* to our survival.

Intuition – Your Key Protector

What happens when you have been given a compliment – one which shows that someone you respect has recognized a special part of you which you may have wanted recognized for a long time? Do you get excited, inspired, feel attractive? Do you have a sudden burst of energy? This is a valuable source of confidence. However, we must be aware that when we lean or rely upon others to make us 'feel good' about ourselves, we are also investing in the possibility of their making us 'feel bad'. One of the first things I learned in aikido was about the danger of unconscious leaning. My teacher pointed out that it is fine to lean upon someone or something so long as there is a mutual agreement; but if you are leaning without knowing it, then you will fall when that person or thing goes away. It is possible to share yourself with another person from a place of feeling whole which will develop once you set a value on yourself.

When we value ourselves, we are in touch with and pay attention to our intuition. One night, some time ago, I was suddenly woken up by a gentle voice from within asking me if I had locked my front door. Feeling somewhat disturbed, I tried to pass it off as a dream. But, within the moments of doubt, there was a flickering memory of my voice in a self-defence class saying, '*Always* listen to that inner voice, especially when it has reference to your safety. This is the voice of your intuition. It is always right.' So, I got up to check the door. It was a good move because, not only had I left it unlocked, it was also ajar. Moments later, while pondering the accuracy of that inner voice, I heard the doorknob being turned – then silence. In the wake of that silence I gave a sigh of relief, knowing I was safe.

I believe my intuition is extremely reliable just because I have cultivated it, given it so much attention that it has become strong enough, tangible enough within me, to trust. Intuition is very much like a plant, animal or child in that it responds qualitatively in accordance with the energy you give to it. If you deny it, it withers. Every time you relate to it with a feeling of love and acceptance, it develops a little more. Most people ask themselves, am I hearing fear, my intuition, or a combination of the two? Wait for a reply. If it is fear, you will remain in a state of fog. If it is your intuition, or a combination of the two, you will either hear your voice telling you what to do, or you will take action, or both.

Stepping Out of the Role of Victim

In my teenage years everyone, including myself, thought that I was one of the most peaceful people around. I never got angry, never showed fear, never expressed sadness except when I saw animals being hurt. Even though I went through some traumatic times, such as the bloody racial riots during my first year in high school while my father was away during the Vietnamese war, and experienced a major earthquake – I showed no emotion. Being the eldest of five children I felt responsible for setting an example – I should be a pillar of strength, always cool and calm – yet I was destroying myself inside with ulcers, arthritis, and the endless silent worry about why all of these things were happening to me.

It was not until a male friend of mine picked me up without my consent and began twirling around with me over his head that I realized how angry and violent I could be. He was having fun: I wasn't. After several ignored pleas to put me back down I became furious. All of the times that I had been hurt or violated in any way – all of those times that I said 'that's all right' when it really wasn't, erupted in a flash and I could hardly believe how angry I was when I saw myself grabbing tenaciously at his windpipe. Even though he threatened to throw me across the room, my senses and my thinking became crystal clear. I called his bluff by informing him that, if he did throw me, his windpipe would go as well because I wasn't going to let go until he put me back on my feet. By this time he was choking and my mother had to pull me off him.

This incident left me with mixed feelings. On one hand, I was pleased to have experienced the enormous power and mental clarity which this righteous anger had released – what a resource! On the other hand, I was afraid of it and felt that it would get out of hand since there was such an apparent backlog of it. Practising judo helped me to channel this force constructively because I could hit the mats while falling and throwing and not hurt anyone. Later, when I began to teach self-defence, I recognized it as a potent source of strength and energy within all of us, especially women because we constantly are aware of the threat of rape, of having our most basic territory violated.

This concern breeds righteous anger and it is our

responsibility, individually and collectively to 'fight back'. There is no dominance without a degree of passivity, and we can help to establish a balance by not permitting violence to rule. We can fight back individually by listening to our intuition, to our feelings and expressing our emotions as clearly as possible first feel them, especially fear and anger.

We can no longer afford to give our strength and power over to those internal messages of self-doubt and hatred. In so doing we are sinking into an unconscious mental suicide, which is simply not necessary when there are other more life-affirming ways we can exist – ways which confirm and strengthen our individual and collective beauty of character and potential. We can begin by occupying more space in the world, by feeling the support of our connection with the earth. Moving this into self-respect for our bodies, our feelings and for positive expression of our emotions – especially fear and anger – we begin to feel our strength. Only then will you have something solid with which you may *stand your ground*.

You stand your ground when you communicate effectively – yes means yes, no means no. We typically have problems saying yes to things which will affirm our power and difficulty in saying no to other people and things which drain it off, mainly because of being conditioned to devalue ourselves. But, individually and collectively, we can recondition ourselves with positive nurturing messages. We don't need to use the approval of society as the yardstick to our expression in the world. This does none of us any good. Perhaps in stepping out of the role as victims or second-rate people we will be inevitable examples to men to break out of some of their restrictive conditioning. By this I am not saying we should grow for the purpose of educating those men who feel the need to abuse and rape women. Quite the contrary, I am saying that we must grow for ourselves *before* we can help others. Likewise, a person cannot truly give without subsequent resentment when there is nothing solid to give from. If women give in order to gain approval for our worth from others, we are caught in a circle of obligation which will ultimately inhibit our ability to receive.

We stand our ground when we recognize the context in which we are operating and stay in touch with our own timing. If you find that you are out of sync with the context, philosophy or people with whom you are involved, then it is up to you to decide whether to expand your ground to embrace something new, or to find a way to meet in the middle. Sometimes the things, people, and places which will help us to grow are not obvious. Through using your intuition, *listening carefully* to your feelings, you will know how to choose. Remember though, it is not always possible or desirable to be out there on the frontier of personal or social expansion. There needs to be a balance between pulling back into yourself, acknowledging and appreciating what you already have, and expanding outwardly. This is a pattern true of the heart beat and of breathing – in-out, in-out. The function is balance. We each have our own way of finding and maintaining balance and it is important to acknowledge this, so that we are not easily caught up into doing what 'everyone else is doing' or what anyone tries to dictate as being right for you.

When we embrace all aspects of what we are, accepting apparent contradictions, they are no longer in opposition to each other but work in harmony. Both extremes of each aspect must be felt fully and an awareness must be cultivated to embrace the fullness of both. Otherwise, if we attach ourselves to one only, the other inevitably gains more power and comes back with even greater force. Such is the case when we feel we must be happy all the time, then crash into sadness; or constantly pleasant, then stored anger disproportionately erupts one day on to something minor; or when we feel we must be in control all the time, then something happens which makes us feel we are helpless.

When we have dreams of monsters, or other exaggerated characters, they are parts of ourselves which we have pushed away. They come back with the degree of energy we have used to push them away. That's why they are so large or distorted. When are we going to stop giving our power away? When will we recognize that deeply seated power comes from embracing both sides of everything? Then, by taking the reins of each into our hands, we can be in charge. We can exert this control and steer our lives in the direction we want by giving up 'the luxury of being weak'.

Individually, we do this by confronting those psychological demons which try to tell us we can't. Perhaps we actually create these demons to goad us into learning about our strength? In any case, we can use them this way rather than seeing them as anonymous assaults on our confidence. You may ask yourself when they appear, 'What is it that I am supposed to be leaving now? What am I supposed to be moving on to?'

FURTHER INFORMATION

By Maggie Comport and Nina Behrman

Having read this book you will not fall into the trap of learning self-defence techniques at classes in a sterile, isolated way: they will be integrated into your whole response to any form of pressure, intrusion or attack. By repeating the exercises in Phases 1 and 2, relating to attitude, physical preparation and actual techniques, you will gain maximum benefit from any in-class training you receive.

You will also get the most out of any classes you attend if you keep yourself in general good health, which could involve the following.

- Devise a light, nutritional, well-balanced diet that suits your physiology and life-style.
- Avoid or cut back on heavy drinking and smoking.
- Take up running, swimming, dancing or a sport such as tennis. As well as improving your general muscle tone and strength, these are aerobic forms of exercise. That is, they increase the efficiency of your respiratory and circulatory system by regularly making them work to capacity.
- Study yoga, which will make your whole body supple, give you breath control, and help you to reach the quiet place inside you (page 25).
- If it isn't possible for you to do any of the above regularly, at least walk (briskly and preferably free of unbalancing weights such as books or shopping) everywhere that you can – including up all stairs and escalators – and do a few limbering and breathing exercises daily at home.

There is an ever-increasing number of self-defence classes available – varying from those that teach martial arts traditionally and can involve a lifetime's interest and commitment, to newer, shorter courses, specifically geared to the needs of women and taught by women. In choosing a course to attend you must consider how much time you can make available and how much you intend to put into studying. At least initially, it is better to do an eight-week course and see it through, hopefully working up from that later, than to start aikido and drop it after three lessons.

You should be prepared to practise some, if not all, the self-defence techniques that you learn between classes, preferably every day. When this is impossible, at least run through the moves in your mind. Although a degree of awareness is better than none, self-defence techniques are not something you can work through once and then put to one side. If they are to serve you well, and your classes are to have a lasting effect, you will need to practise the techniques always. They then become an integral part of your life, second nature, something with which you won't want to lose touch.

Going to a course that has been recommended by a friend is a good idea: going with several friends is even better – it provides an incentive to attend regularly, you can practise with each other in between, and they can fill you in if you do have to miss a class.

When you start classes you must use your own judgement as to how much the particular philosophy and techniques suit your personality and needs. After making an initial effort to overcome any difficulties you may experience, if you then don't like the teacher personally, or disagree with the attitudes being imparted, or find the techniques alien, leave and try something different.

If you are not totally happy with the class, but have limited or no choice because of where you live or when you can attend, then stay with the classes, absorbing what does suit you and rejecting what doesn't. Perhaps at the end of the course you might like to take up with the teacher the points you disagree with, and why: the whole class may wish to discuss certain aspects of their course – either in the class or, if that is getting nowhere, outside.

If you really don't like the classes you can get to, or nothing at all is available, consider asking some individual or body to set some up, first making sure that the teachers are qualified and insured. If you want to work as a group with a teacher it is possible to devise and communicate your own techniques.

Self-Defence Courses – What to Look For

Before enrolling for any course in self-defence you should satisfy yourself about the way the course is conducted, the competence of the teacher/s, the safety and suitability of the premises where classes are held, and check you will be covered by adequate insurance, provided by either the course organizers or yourself. Compare the prices of private courses.

It is important to discover the thinking behind a course, whether it deals solely with physical techniques or also with the philosophy of self-preservation and the broader issues of women and violence, so that you can decide whether the course is appropriate to your needs. And it is useful to find out not only what body or individual is providing the course but with whom teachers have trained and to what level.

Control of Women's Self-Defence Courses

The majority of women who come to self-defence courses have personal experience of violence, abuse, assault, intimidation or harassment. When courses are taught by women the teachers are able to relate directly to the experience of the women who come to them, and a lot of discussion, sharing and feedback goes on. This articulation and airing process contributes to women's growth, feelings of self-validation, ideas for techniques and determination to resist attacks.

Specially designed courses which are run by women for women are controlled in several ways, and it is possible to provide only a selection of contacts in the following pages. But these bodies should be able to provide information on the availability of local women's self-defence courses, as well as details of teachers' training. Many of the teachers have a traditional martial arts background but have moved on to self-defence for women.

- independent individuals and groups of women self-defence teachers, in the employ of any of the below or operating privately
- Workers' Education Associations
- Local Education Authorities and/or local government
- Rape Crisis Centres, Women's Aid, Incest Survivors' Groups, Women's Centres

Where no suitable courses are available, get together with other women and ask one of the above to start or become involved in organizing courses.

Independent Teachers

A growing number of groups of women self-defence teachers have set up their own courses and teacher training programmes and had their work officially recognized by WEAs or LEAs.

Certain women self-defence teachers in Braitin have actually been trained in depth by Khaleghl Quinn or one of her authorized teachers. Khaleghl's Quindo Centre which trains both students and teachers can supply a list of accredited teachers.

There are other qualified women self-defence teachers who have developed their own physical techniques along the lines of Khaleghl's, and are in sympathy with her philosophy on self-preservation, though they do not use the names Khaleghl Quinn, Stand Your Ground or Self-Preservation to describe their courses, and Khaleghl is quite happy that they include elements of her work in their teaching. There are yet other teachers who are using the above names to describe their courses, though they have not qualified with Khaleghl.

London

The Quindo Centre
2 West Heath Drive
London NW11 7QH
Tel: 081 455 8698

Belfast

c/o Women's Education
 Project
143a University Street
Belfast BT7 1HP
Tel: 0232 230212

Birmingham Women's Self-Defence Group

c/o Peta Jackson
18 Towyn Road
Moseley
Birmingham 13 9NA
Tel: 021 777 8470

Glasgow

Glasgow Women's Self-
 Defence Group
c/o Women's Support
 Project
Newlands Centre
871 Springfield Road
Glasgow G31 4HQ
Tel: 041 554 5669

Hull

Hull Women's Centre
1st Floor Queen's Dock
 Chambers
Queen's Dock Avenue
Hull HU1 3DR
Tel: 0482 226806

Newcastle

c/o Them Wifies
109 Pilgrim Street
Newcastle upon Tyne
 NE1 6QF
Tel: 091 261 4090

Workers' Educational Association

The WEA is an independent body, receiving grants from the Department of Education and Science and LEAs. It is divided nationally into nineteen districts, organized in local branches. Some districts run self-defence courses, taught by women for women, and usually in sympathy with Khaleghl Quinn's aims, and WEAs are starting to train their own teachers. Some branches work particularly closely with the LEA. For contacts, look in your phone book, or ask the national office.

WEA National Office
Temple House
17 Victoria Park Square
London E2 9PB
Tel: 081 983 1515

Local Authorities

Recreation departments which set up self-defence courses for women may be unaware of what is good practice in such courses or unable to find suitably trained teachers. At sports and community centres it is common to employ high-graded (usually male) martial arts specialists to teach self-defence courses, and women may not feel comfortable with these teachers, nor find their wider concerns about women and violence considered.

Where the LEA sets up courses, the position is likely to be more favourable. There is a growing emphasis on women's studies plus an increased understanding of how widespread violence to women is and how necessary special self-defence courses by women for women are. Some Adult Education Institutes, universities, colleges and schools now run such courses in addition to traditional martial arts courses. In a few cases LEAs train teachers themselves.

District Councils nationwide and London Boroughs (inner and outer) can provide information on local courses. The 'Searchlight' directory details all adult education classes and courses held in Inner London. It is published every Autumn, and is available from newsagents and at public libraries.

Specific Needs

Courses that are variously funded but usually contactable through a women's centre are run for women who feel doubly endangered and want help from those who understand their particular perspective on violence. In one London survey over half of the Black women questioned had been verbally abused and over a quarter actually assaulted because of their race, and lesbian women, women with disabilities and older women often find they are special targets.

Lesbian and Gay Switchboard
Tel: 01 837 7324
24 hour service

MAC-1 Courses

The Martial Arts Commission (page 161) became

concerned that self-defence was being taught badly and without adequate controls, so stepped in with a specially created course, drawing on a range of martial arts. MAC-1 is designed for people of average fitness who have little interest in martial arts but 'do have considerable interest in wanting to learn some techniques of a simple and effective nature to defend themselves against physical aggression'. MAC-1 does not cover the specific needs of women, avoidance or assertiveness. The course lasts 15-18 weeks, instructors (usually male) have an MAC-1 coach's award (four levels), and insurance is included in the fee.

The MAC has not run MAC-1 for several years, although there are plans to start it up again in the future. The MAC is currently undergoing organisational changes, and a course similar to MAC-1 may be established outside the organisation, possibly at several regional centres throughout the UK, by:

Eddy Stratton

Meadowside, Northdown Road
Slade, Bideford
North Devon EX39 3LX
Tel: 0237 476774

Police Self-Defence Courses

If you want to get together a group of women, privately or through your place of work, and approach your local police station, they can usually provide an officer to teach a short, free self-defence course. Courses consist of, say, four sessions of two hours each; some include slides and videos and cover attention to personal safety. The group will need to organize premises, mats, and their own insurance. Everyone attending has to sign an indemnity form.

Further information from:

Tina Joyce

Albany Street Police Station
60 Albany Street
London NW1 4EE
Tel: 071 725 4212

Self-Defence in Martial Arts

Martial arts training takes place at a physical, mental and philosophical level. It improves fitness, alertness, co-ordination, and is intended to sublimate aggression and instil discipline – all of which will help you in self-defence. Some forms teach armed and unarmed combat, but all provide a self-defence system, which varies according to the art.

The Martial Arts Commission is a governing body, recognized by the Sports Council, local authorities and police chiefs. Apart from judo, which is an Olympic sport with its own organization, the MAC control and coordinate what goes on in the martial arts in Britain and offer information and contacts. They 'do not believe that they have the monopoly on true martial art but are able to underwrite those in membership'.

They offer strict guidelines and recommendations to those teaching martial arts and or self-defence. These cover the competence and social responsibility of instructors, the suitability of students, the size of classes, the choice and running of premises, and adequate insurance cover. To guarantee the proficiency of coaches, the MAC's federal members endorse individual licences.

Martial Arts Commission
1st Floor Broadway House
15-16 Deptford Broadway
London SE8 4PE
Tel: 081 691 8711

British Judo Association
7a Rutland Street
Leicester LE1 1RB
Tel: 0533 559 669

Avoiding Confrontation

However disciplined you are, no amount of training will make you invincible – it is still better not to have to defend yourself than to have to take on an attacker or attackers. Galling as it is for women to accept limitations – *why shouldn't* we go about our business when and how we choose, free from fear – society is not going to change overnight, and there is no sense in making yourself an unnecessarily easy target.

Apart from being unjust, it is quite useless to tell women to stay off the streets. We have to work, attend meetings and have a right to entertainment and a social life – all of which will at some time involve being out late in the dark. Many women live alone and, anyway, partners and flatmates, whether male or female, cannot always be on call. Because of their financial position far from all women own or have priority access to a car, or even a motorbike or moped. Some women can't even afford to use the poor and irregular public transport facilities that do exist and are forced to walk home through dark and dangerous streets (which is why good public transport is very much the concern of women). Even if you do have a car, or take a taxi run by a reputable operator late at night, there is frequently a time between leaving a vehicle and entering a building when you are vulnerable to a concealed attacker.

Given the inevitability of sometimes being out alone late or being at home alone, it is still possible to improve your chances of avoiding attack.

On the street

- Don't ignore anything you think just *might* mean danger: assume it does and react accordingly.
- However cold and tired you are, don't walk along with shoulders rounded, head down, eyes on the pavement, ears muffled up. Stay alert and *look* alert. Use your peripheral vision all the time, listen carefully, and keep your senses finely tuned.
- To avoid unlit, deserted streets, be prepared to walk the long way round.
- Using a torch can be very dangerous: you are visible, but cannot see past its limited pool of light. It is better to accustom your eyes to the dark.
- Walking on the outside of the pavement to stay clear of doorways and alleyway entrances may be best – but watch out that a car doesn't glide up behind you so that occupants can grab you.
- If you are being followed and see a pub, service station or other public premises open, go in and phone the police and/or a friend. Also tell the publican, cashier or anyone else likely to help you.
- Don't rely on people coming to your aid if you yell for help, even if they can see you being attacked. If you can make it plain that you don't know the man or men concerned you may get assistance. If it is possible, break away and run into a group containing women.
- Be prepared to yell and bang on doors of lit houses if you think you are going to be attacked. Don't, however, assume that someone will take notice – you might be better off running straight away.
- Yelling 'Fire!' arouses people's self-interest and curiosity and gets a better response than crying the traditional 'Help!'
- Carry your keys on your person, not in your bag, especially if your name and/or address are unavoidably in your bag. If you were robbed and/or beaten up, being locked out of your home would be the last straw. If your keys are stolen along with your name and/or address,

you *must* change your lock/s immediately. If they are stolen alone and you can afford to change the lock, do so; your assailant may know where you live, anyway.

• In the street, leave your hands free. Wherever possible, carry nothing – this might also make you less of a target to a robber. If you have to transport some things, try to use a bag that will go over your shoulder.

• Think about what you carry. Don't take anything bulky, awkward or heavy when you don't have to; anything of sentimental value, irreplaceable information, personal documents you don't need on that trip, excess money, cheque books and bank or credit cards if you don't need them that day, unnecessary correspondence and forms of identification. In that way, you will be less physically encumbered if you are attacked, and won't hesitate to jettison your bag if necessary.

• If you are very determined not to part company with your bag, use either a small one slung across your body under a jacket or coat, or a shoulder bag with a short, strong strap and good fastenings. Make sure it sits close to your body with the fastenings innermost.

• Wear shoes in which you can at least walk swiftly, preferably run in: they should be secure and give good balance. Or wear ones that you are prepared to kick off and abandon in order to defend yourself or run. You may feel it is important to be able to move silently as well, and pick your footwear accordingly.

• Avoid garments that will impede your movements; skirts that stop you running or kicking; bits and pieces that can be used to restrain or strangle you.

Accepting lifts

Accepting a lift from a man, even if there is only the driver in the car, is potentially very dangerous, especially in a car with centrally locking doors under the driver's control. The police implore women not to accept lifts under any circumstances, so don't expect any official sympathy if you end up in trouble.

Public transport

• If possible, walk on from a very isolated bus-stop to a more frequented one.

• Try to sit near other women, or the driver, on an open bus, or guard on an underground train.

• If someone bothers you at all, make a fuss straight away – don't wait until he has you alone.

• On a train, don't be afraid to pull the emergency cord.

Driving on your own
- Always lock a car carefully when leaving it.
- On returning, check the inside to see no one is hiding in there, even if the doors were locked.
- Have your keys to hand so you do not fiddle about.
- Sitting in a car – waiting or driving – check all the doors are locked: in an old car, wind down the driver's window and lock it from outside with the key.
- Keep windows shut or almost shut: use any quarter lights for ventilation.
- If you think you are being followed, drive to the nearest police station.
- Don't give lifts to men.
- Give any women walking on their own a lift.
- Do not stop to help a stranded motorist. Drive to the next telephone and call for assistance.

Public places
Use caution in conversation with, or overheard by, male strangers. Avoid giving your name, address or place of employment or revealing that you live alone.

At home
- Use only your initials and surname on your doorbell and in the phone book.
- A Yale-type lock can be easily opened: fit a deadbolt lock to BS 3621. Ensure that the door and frame are adequate at these points.
- Fit a spyhole or ask any callers to identify themselves.
- Fit a door chain and use it.
- All windows should be secured before you go out, and accessible ones while you are in.
- Draw curtains or blinds after dark.
- Don't admit anyone unknown without formal identification.
- Should a stranger ask to use your phone, don't let them in but offer to make the call yourself.
- If you hear strange noises outside your home, call the police.
- When you get near your home doorway, look up and down the street, stairs or corridor before taking out your keys and standing in front of your door. Don't fiddle around at the door, all concentration on unlocking: stay alert and get inside as quickly as possible.
- Should you return home to find doors or windows tampered with, leave immediately. Call the police from a neighbour's or the nearest callbox.
- If you are at home and think you have an intruder,

get straight out if you can. Break a window to call attention if you have to.

What The Community Can Do

By consulting with people in your area – authorities, neighbours, other women – it is possible to reduce opportunities for being attacked. The following suggestions come from the London Rape Crisis Centre leaflet *Rape And Fighting Back*.

- If the lighting on your street, block of flats, estate or college is poor, keep lobbying your landlord, council or college authorities until something is done about it.
- Kerb-crawlers can be dealt with by publishing their car registration numbers in a leaflet and handing it out to women in the area.
- If there have been a lot of attacks or rapes in your area, call a public meeting and discuss:

a escorting or transporting women to their homes if they work or attend classes after dark

b arranging an alarm system to alert local residents, such as whistles

c getting to know immediate neighbours and arranging an agreed alarm system

d making a rota for picking up children from schools

e compiling a list of attacks that have taken place with facts about time, place, attacker, which can be published in a newsletter and/or given to the police

f ensuring that the local police are taking the problem seriously and are treating raped women with respect

g if judges have made contemptuous remarks or decisions, picketing their courts, homes or places of worship

h if a man has attacked or raped but not been arrested, and if the woman concerned agrees, circulating a 'wanted' poster with his photograph and description

Helpful and Campaigning Organizations

If you have been attacked, or suffered in a violent relationship, or know someone who needs help; or if you wish to become involved in offering support to other women, or working for changes in the law and society's attitudes to violence to women (page 174), you can contact these organizations.

Rape Crisis Centres

These centres give a free, confidential service to girls and women. They offer practical advice, medical and legal information; emotional support immediately following an attack, together with someone to accompany you if you wish to report the incident to the police or go to a doctor or clinic treating sexually transmitted diseases or abortion clinic, or later have to attend court; or the chance to talk over something that happened to you at some time in the past, including childhood experiences.

In order to re-establish the control and power that is taken away by the act of rape, it helps to share the distress and burden by talking about how you feel in an environment where you will be believed and supported. If you have been sexually assaulted or raped – by a stranger or by someone you know – and need help, you can get in touch with any RCC. If you phone during the hours shown you will be able to speak with a woman there, and many centres operate a twenty-four hour answering service on which you can leave a message, or ask for the address and write.

Aberdeen 0224 575560 Mon 6-8pm; Thu 7-9pm; 24 hour answering
Antrim 084 94 65256 Fri and Sat 5.30-7.30pm
Bangor 0248 354885 Wed 7-9pm
Belfast 0232 249696; 0232 321830 Mon-Fri l0am-6pm; Sat 11am-5pm, 24 hour answering
Birmingham 021 766 5366; 021 766 5539 (office) 24 hour counselling
Bradford 0274 308270 Mon l-5pm; Wed noon-3pm; Thu 6-10pm; 24 hour answering
Brighton 0273 203733 Tues 6-9pm; Fri 3-9pm; Sat l0am-lam; 24 hour answering
Bristol 0272 428331 Mon-Fri 10.30am-2.30pm; 24 hour answering
Cambridge 0223 358314 Wed 6-midnight; Sat 11am-5pm; 24 hour answering
Canterbury 0227 450400 6-9pm every evening
Cardiff 0222 373181 Mon and Thu 7-10pm; Wed 11am-2pm; 24 hour answering
Chelmsford 0245 492123 Fri 7.30-9.30pm
Cleveland 0642 225787 Mon-Thu l0am-3pm; Thu 7.30-10.30pm; 24 hour answering
Cork 010 353 21 968086 Mon 7.30-10pm; Wed 2-5pm; Fri l0am-lpm; Sat 10-4pm; 24 hour answering
Coventry 0203 677229 Mon-Fri 11am-3pm; 24 hour answering
Croydon 081 688 0332 Tues 7-10pm; Sat 3-6pm
Cumbria 0228 36500 Mon 1.30-4pm; Wed 7-10pm; 24 hour answering
Derby 0332 372545 Thu 7.30-9.30pm; 24 hour answering
Dorset 0305 772295; 24 hour answering
Dublin 010 353 161 4911; 24 hour counselling
Dundee 0382 201291 Wed 7-9pm
Edinburgh 031-556 9437 Mon and Fri 12-2pm; Tue 6-8pm; Thu 7-10pm; 24 hour answering
Exeter 0392 430 871 Mon-Fri l0am-5pm; 24 hour answering
Falkirk 0324 38433 Mon 7-9pm
Galway 010 353 91 64983 24 hour answering
Gloucester 0452 526770 Mon 7.30-9.30pm; Thu 11.30am-2pm; 24 hour answering
Grays Thurrock 0375 380609; 0375 381322 (office) Mon 7-10 pm;

Wed l-5pm, Thu noon-4pm; 24 hour answering
Hull 0482 29990 Thu 4-midnight
Inverness 0463 220719 Mon, Thu, Sat and Sun 7-10pm
Lancaster 0524 382595 Tue 7.30-9.30pm; Fri 1-3pm
Leamington 0926 39936 Mon 11am-3pm and 7-9pm; 24 hour answering
Leeds 0532 440058; 0532 441323 (office) Mon-Sun noon-4pm; Mon-Fri 7-10pm
Leicester 0533 706990; 0533 702977 (office) Tues 7-10pm; Sat 2-5pm
Letterkenny 010 353 74 23067 Mon l0am-noon; Sat noon-4pm
Limerick 010 353 61 41211 Mon-Fri l0am-4pm; 24 hour answering
Liverpool 051-727 7599 Mon 7-9pm; Thu and Sat 2-5pm; 24 hour answering
London 071-837 1600; 071 916 5466 (office) 24 hour counselling
Luton 0582 33592; 0582 33426 (office) Mon-Fri 9am-5pm; Sat l0am-noon
Manchester 061-834 8784; 061 839 8379 Tues and Fri 2-5pm; Wed, Thu and Sun 6-9pm; 24 hour answering
Medway 0634 811 703 24 hour answering
Milton Keynes 0908 670312 Mon 7-9pm; 24 hour answering
North Staffordshire 0782 204177 24 hour counselling
Norwich 0603 667687 Mon 6-8pm; Thu 8-10pm; Sat 4-6pm; 24 hour answering
Nottingham 0602 410440 Tues-Fri l0am-4pm; Sat l0am-lpm
Oxford 0865 726295 Mon and Tues 7-9pm; Thu and Fri 2-4pm; Wed 2-10pm; 24 hour answering
Peterborough 0733 340515 Tues 7.30-10pm; Sat l0am-noon
Plymouth 0752 23584 Thu 7.30-10pm
Portsmouth 0705 669511 Wed and Sat 7-10pm; Fri 7pm-7am; 24 hour answering
Reading 0734 55577 Sun 7.30-10pm; 24 hour answering
Rochdale 0706 526279 Mon-Thu 8-10pm; 24 hour answering
Scunthorpe 0724 853953 Mon 7-9pm
Sheffield 0742 755255 Mon and Fri 11am-4pm; Tues 7-9pm; 24 hour answering
Southampton 0703 701213 Mon 7-10pm; Tue l0am-lpm; Thu 1-4pm; 24 hour answering
Strathclyde 041-221 8448 Mon, Wed and Fri 7-10pm; 24 hour answering
Swansea 0792 648805 Tues 7-9pm; Fri 10-12 noon
Tyneside 091-232 9858 Mon-Fri l0am-5pm; Sat and Sun 6.30-10pm; 24 hour answering
Waterford 010 353 51 73362 No fixed time; 24 hour answering
Wirral 051-666 1392 Thu 7-9pm; Sun 2-5pm

Women's Aid

Women, and their children, who are suffering violence in a domestic relationship can seek help and information about housing, their legal position and social security, or find a place in a refuge, through WA offices. The phone number of your local office or a volunteer who can help you should be in the phone book; if not, get in touch with your Citizens' Advice Bureau. In most cases the number provides contact twenty-four hours a day. The addresses of refuges are not published – this is to protect the residents. WAs publish a number of helpful booklets and information kits. They also work to remind people of the existence of battering and to campaign for changes in attitudes as well as in the laws and social practices which affect battered women.

Women's Aid

52 Featherstone Street
London EC1Y 8RT
Tel: 071 251 6537

Child Abuse

If you have been forced into a sexual relationship by a male relative or friend of the family, are being subjected to sexual attentions by them, have any fears or suspicions about their behaviour to you, or are being beaten and illtreated, you *do not* have to put up with this treatment. *Don't* keep things to yourself. There is no reason to feel guilty or ashamed, because it is the man or boy who is doing something very wrong and your problem is an extremely common one. In America one quarter of all women are thought to be sexually abused before they are eighteen, mostly by someone they know. In Northumbria, women doctors working with the police have found that 82% of rape victims they see are under sixteen and 27% were less than six years old.

You may find it impossible to tell your mother, about your own plight or that of a younger sister, so try talking to another female relative or teacher that you feel close to. If you want to talk anonymously to someone who knows how you feel, contact one of the following. If you are grown-up but have been abused in the past, or have discovered child abuse in your family, they can help you also.

Brook Advisory Centres

24-hour automated helpline:
 071 410 0420
153a East Street
London SE17 2SD
Tel: 071 708 1234
or see phone book for local
 branches

Childline

Freephone 24-hour helpline:
 0800 1111

NSPCC

Freephone 24-hour helpline:
 0800 800500

Rape Crisis Centres

see pages 166-7

Social Services

see phone book under local council's name

Women's Aid Refuges

see phone book under Women's Aid

Youth Advisory Centres

see phone book

What To Do If You Have Been Attacked

The following information and advice is taken from Rape Crisis Centre leaflets.

The legal definition of rape is:
'The unlawful carnal knowledge of a female by force or fraud against her will.' Carnal knowledge means penetration of the labia (outer lips of the vagina) by the penis to any degree – full penetration and ejaculation need not take place in order to prove rape.

It can involve:
- intimidation with threats or weapons
- beating, choking, knifing
- sexual and mental humiliation
- urination, defaecation or spitting on the victim
- forced oral sex
- forced anal sex
- injury to genitals by bottles, sticks, etc being pushed up the vagina
- extensive soreness, internal bruising, lacerations and bleeding of the genitals due to forced penetration when the woman is in a terrorized and resistant state
- multiple rape by one or more assailants

It is likely that:
- the assailant will be a man you trust (about 60%)
- you will be raped in your own home (about 50%)
- the rape will be accompanied by other forms of sexual assault or abuse and the use of weapons (30%)

If you decide to report to the police:
NB This is entirely your decision – RCCs will support whatever decision you make.

- Report to the police as soon as possible – delay may go against you.
- If at all possible, tell someone what has happened as soon as you can – a witness to your distress and early complaint will help.
- Do not wash, tidy yourself or change clothing – you may destroy valuable medical evidence.
- Do not take any alcohol or drugs.
- Call a friend or RCC so that someone can give you support during police and medical procedures.
- Take a change of warm clothing with you to the station – the police may keep some or all of your original clothing for tests and evidence.
- Making notes may help you when you make your statement: important things to remember are sequence of events, details and what was said.

- See your own doctor at suitable intervals to check for the development of bruising (to be added to the evidence), any form of sexually transmitted disease, pregnancy. If you subsequently suffer from nightmares, insomnia, psychological or sexual problems, inform your doctor. You will at least have further evidence of the distress you have been caused.

Whether or not you report to the police:
- talk to someone about what has happened – you need friendship at this time
- see a doctor to check for any form of sexually transmitted disease, pregnancy, possible injury

Reactions

Whatever reaction you have to rape or sexual assault, whether it is anger, calm or fear, it is right for you – there is no standard reaction. The most important thing is to trust your feelings and talk to someone about it.

Police Procedure

You will be at the station for several hours, during which the following will take place:

- You will be asked to make a written statement which will be taken down by a police officer. Make sure you read it carefully and change it if necessary before you sign it. You can ask to make a statement to a woman police officer.
- You will be asked intimate questions: there is no reason why you should talk to any officer other than the one in charge of your case.
- To collect evidence of rape or sexual assault a medical examination, external and internal, will be made, hopefully in a proper victim suite. You can ask for a woman doctor or your own GP.
- You may be asked to look at mug shots, accompany the police to the scene of the crime, or identify your assailant/s.
- You can ask for it to be noted that you don't want your name read out in court.
- If you feel you are not being well treated, ask to see the officer in charge of the station.
- Damages can be awarded by the courts or you may apply to the Criminal Injuries Compensation Board, so ask the police for details.

Pregnancy

If you have been raped and were not protected by being

on the pill or having an IUD you must consider the chance that you have become pregnant. (The London RCC say that about 13% of rapes they deal with result in known pregnancies – they couldn't follow up on almost half the women so the figure may be higher.) If you don't want to wait for a pregnancy test (until your next period is due) and want to avoid an abortion, you could seek post-coital contraception. This is available in two forms: hormonal pills (to be taken within seventy-two hours, preferably within forty-eight hours); or insertion of an intra-uterine device (can be fitted up to five days after unprotected intercourse). Some clinics offer early pregnancy tests.

It should be possible in most areas to get post-coital or emergency contraception free of charge, within the National Health Service, from your local GP or family planning clinic. This service is also available from other organisations such as the British Pregnancy Advisory Service or the Pregnancy Advisory Service for a fee (£30 and £25 respectively). See your local phone book for branches in your area.

Working for Change

One way of furthering our self-preservation is to work for change in public attitudes, structures in society that perpetuate our oppression, and laws relating to violence and intimidation directed at females.

Rape and Sexual Assault

The current definition of rape is very limited and women are campaigning:
- to extend the definitions in law and practice to include attempted rape; forced oral or anal sex; the use of objects for sexual violation; urination and defaecation
- for the attacker to be charged with all the related crimes (drugging, beating up, abduction)
- for consent no longer to be equated with submission and decided on the presence or absence of physical injury; and for it to be insufficient for the man to argue subjectively that he believed the woman consented
- criminalization of rape by males under fourteen

Certain police forces have started to make efforts to give credibility to women's reports of sexual assault and rape and to respond with sensitivity. Beneficial changes have included; allowing victims to have a constant companion; initially taking only a brief statement; special suites for interviews and medical examinations; conducting examinations at a clinic and involving women doctors; using one specially trained female officer to deal with each report; limiting questions to the strictly relevant; providing printed information; preserving anonymity.

However, about half of women who report attacks say they are not happy with the police response. While this continues, and until women feel the police and judiciary accept they do not lie about sex attacks, and that these acts are serious, they will remain under-reported and their prevalence grossly under-estimated by society. At the moment 70-90% of women who consult RCCs do not want to report their experience, and statistics show part of the reason why.

- In Scotland in 1985 of 248 rapes made known to the police, 80 men were prosecuted, 39 proved guilty, and 15 received sentences of over five years.
- In England and Wales in 1984, 16,000 sex offences were recorded but only 1,300 offenders over 21 sentenced to immediate imprisonment.

The process of reporting continues the loss of control imposed by the assault. Women do not realize their status is only chief witness for the prosecution or that in court they will be virtually in the role of defendant. Improvements being suggested are:

- remove the burden of proof from victim
- give victim separate representation and keep her informed at all stages
- reduce delays in hearings (currently 6-9 months)
- protect victim from coming face to face with attacker/s
- with all sex offences ensure victim's name is not read out in court and media do not identify her in any way
- do not permit raising in court of sexual history or orientation (this is still being introduced without application to judge, or 75% of applications allowed)
- no reduction in charge in return for guilty plea
- admissibility of video evidence from victim
- address issue of racism throughout police and judiciary and links between racial and sexual assaults
- increase recruitment of women into police, legal profession and judiciary, plus make special training compulsory for all involved
- introduce uniform sentences that reflect the gravity of the attacks

Domestic Violence

This is still seen as a private matter but improvements in the law and how it is enforced can have an effect. For example, in Canada home arrests of violent males have lowered the incidence of battering. Putting the onus on the state, not women, to prosecute protects them from their partners' pressure to drop charges. Laws governing the matrimonial home have been improved but more funds are needed for rehousing (temporary and permanent) while relevant social security payments have actually got worse.

As with sex offences, some police forces have been making efforts to respond more sensitively and positively to reports of domestic violence, but much remains to be done. Although the Metropolitan police, for example, receive over 1,000 calls a week for assistance in such incidents, about 75% go unreported. In a survey done in one part of London, of 450 reports of domestic violence only 2% reached court. Changes put forward by concerned organizations are:

- all physical injury to be the subject of a crime report
- police to keep adequate records on domestic disputes
- specialist training to be provided
- women interpreters to be provided where necessary
- officers not to attempt reconciliation
- victims to be interviewed away from attackers
- printed information to be provided
- police to be more prepared to charge offenders, using their various existing powers
- victims to be informed when men are to be released
- women who are no longer cohabiting to be able to get injunctions
- powers of arrest to be attached to all court orders
- arrest to be mandatory not discretionary
- prison sentences to be imposed for breaking orders
- state prosecution to bring proceedings to underline seriousness of offence, not act as mediator

Child Abuse

Because so many laws cover the violent and sexual abuse of children, including incest, rationalization is urgently required – partly to help reveal more clearly the extent and type of abuse. Child abuse has close links with domestic violence and sexual assaults generally and, like them, is widely under-reported. While teaching children that they have a right to be free from fear and molestation, to say no, may help them to tell someone, that is no good if they are treated as liars in court. And it should always be clear that responsibility lies solely with the males who commit these crimes. Recent humanization of procedures is welcome but should be speeded up as it is vital for children who already feel scared and guilty about telling to feel protected at all stages.

Pornography

Sexual behaviour is learned and pornography (as distinct from erotic, sexually explicit materials premised on equality) provides the 'education', distortion of sexual arousal to connect it with pain, suffering and humiliation of the female, and permission for males to act as if sexual assault, rape and violence are acceptable – even what women want. There is a growing will to counter the abuse of women and children through pornography by making it illegal, but not, as has traditionally been attempted, on the grounds that it is obscene.

Pornographic representation of women could be said to constitute a massive defamation on their reputation and one move is to get it recognized as a form of libel. Another way of viewing pornography is as incitement to hatred. Incitement to racial hatred is already illegal, so there is a precedent for extending the law on the grounds that pornography infringes the civil liberties of women and children. There is also a wish to see media reporting of sex offences and the way women are represented in the media and advertising better controlled.

What to Do

To get involved in campaigning for improvements you can contact your local RCC, WA, councillors, women's committee, branches of women's groups, trade unions or political parties or your MP. You can write letters, draw up petitions, pass resolutions, speak at meetings, or on local radio. If you cannot get information locally, contact:

House of Commons
London SW1A 0AA
Tel: 071 219 3000

Sexual Violence and the Law

c/o Rights of Women
52-54 Featherstone Street
London EC1Y 8RT
Tel: 071 251 6577

Women Against Violence Against Women
c/o Rights of Women
52-54 Featherstone Street
London EC1Y 8RT
Tel: 071 251 6577

NB While every care has been taken to ensure that all information given in this section is correct at the time of going to press, the author and publishers cannot be held responsible for any changes that subsequently occur.

Key Addresses

UK

The Quindo Centre
2 West Heath Drive
London
NW11 7QH
Tel: 081 455 8698

USA

Quindo International Ltd
PO Box 7178
San Bernardino
California 92411

INDEX

abortion 171
accepting lifts 163
advisory centres 172
aikido 18–19
air, element of 61, 65
arm: elbow-back 126
    press-ups 45
    resilient arm exercise 17–19
    underarm pin 106–7
armed attack 136–41
assertion 149

back: knife at 140
    lower back toning 140
birth control, post-coital 171
blending 92
body escapes 86–9
body weapons 74–85

calf stretches 71
chest, relaxation of 48
chokes 97–100
    from behind 98–9
    from front 100
classes, self-defence 155–6
    see also courses
clawing 127
courses, self-defence for women 156–61

double finger poke 128
driving alone 164

earth, element of 38–9, 60–1, 63
elbow back 126
elements 38–9, 60–5, 89–90
emotional bondage 61–2
evasions 86–90
eyes: double finger poke 128
    pushing into skull 129

falls 109–15
    over the shoulder roll 114
    side sweep 112
    triangular forward break 113
    wilting flower 111
feinting 81–2
fire, element of 61, 64–5
fist, making a 124
follow-through 91–2

grips 93–6
    cross-wrist 94–5
    double-wrist 96
    single-hand 93
groin: groin throw 134
    kick or knee to 121
grounding exercises 40–4
group attacks 108

hand, heel of 126
    making a fist 124
handstands 72
head: back of head strike 129
health, general 155
heel of hand thrust 126
hip throw 131
holds 91–108
    see also chokes, grips, pins
home, attacks in 167–9
home security 164–5

impact 83
incest 168–9
    advisory services 169
intuition 21–5, 151

judo 161

kicks 116–21
    backward 119
    front snap 118
    side 120
    to groin 121
knee bends 71
knives 136–41
    at throat from behind 141
    at your back 140
    brandishing 138–9
    lying down attack 141

legs: calf stretches 71
    grounding exercises 40–4
    inner leg hook 132
    inner leg reap 135
    knee bends 71

martial arts 55, 77
    governing bodies 161
    self-defence courses 160
meditation 26
mental attitude 15–17
mental barriers 49
myths 51

nurturing guide 58–9

physical contact 35–7
pillow punching 83
pins 101–7
    four-point frustration 104–5
    on stomach 102–3
    side-choking 106–7
    underarm 106–7
police, reporting rape to 148–9, 170–71
pregnancy 171–2
    advisory services 172
press-ups 44–50, 72

public transport 163–4
punching 125
    pillow punching 83

quiet place, the 25–6

rape 145, 169–71
    campaigning groups 166–9
    crisis centres 166–7
    reporting to police 148–9, 170–71
relaxation 25–6, 48
resilient arm exercise 17–19
responses, unconventional 27–30

self-defence courses 156–61
self-hatred 56–9
self-worth 20–1
shoulder: roll 114
    throw 133
sit-ups, half 72
stamina 69
street, safety in 162–3
strength, resilient 17–19
strikes, upper body 122–9

target areas 75–6
throat: chokes 98–100
    knife at 141
throws 130–5
    groin throw 134
    hip throw 131
    inner leg hook 132
    inner leg reap 135
    over shoulder throw 133
tiger claw 127

ungrounding exercise 42
upper body strikes 122–9

violence 52, 146
voice, power of 84–5

water, element of 61, 63–4
weapons 53–5
    body weapons 74–85
well-being programme 71–3
where to strike 78–9
wives, battered 150, 167–8
women's organisations 166–9

yoga 155